HISTORY OF THE WORLD
THE STUDY GUIDE

Second PRINTING
COPYRIGHT © 2009 VISION FORUM MINISTRIES
All Rights Reserved

"Where there is no vision, the people perish." (Proverbs 29:18)

Vision Forum Ministries
4719 Blanco Rd., San Antonio, Texas 78212
www.visionforumministries.org

Compiled by Elijah Brown

Typography by Justin Turley

All Scripture taken from the King James Version

PRINTED IN THE UNITED STATES OF AMERICA

This Study Guide is dedicated to Henry R. Van Til, whose book,

The Calvinistic Concept of Culture, forever reminds us that history

and culture are unmerited products of God's sovereign grace.

TABLE of CONTENTS

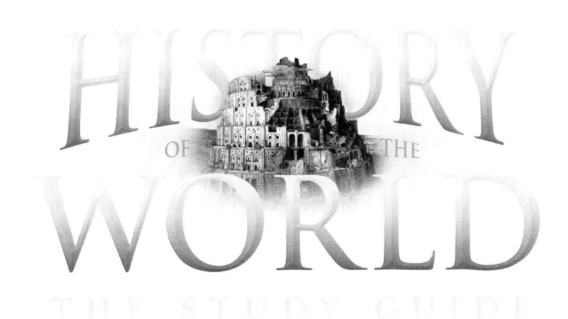

HISTORY

OF THE

WORLD

THE STUDY GUIDE

CHAPTER I

ORIGINS AND THE BIBLICAL FRAMEWORK OF HISTORY

INTRODUCTION

"In the beginning God created the heavens and the earth." It is this event described in Genesis 1:1 that marks the beginning of our study of world history. The opening chapter of Genesis not only provides the historian with the only reliable account of historical creation, but it also provides the student of history with the foundation and framework for all other historical inquiries.

From the opening verses of Scripture, we discover that the study of history is inseparably linked to the study of theology. In fact, the best theologies written to date have been propped up on two main inquiries: the study of God (theology proper), and His relation with the universe (history). Reformed theologian Herman Bavinck explains further that:

> *From the very first moment, true religion distinguishes itself from all other religions by the fact that it construes the relation between God and the World, including man, as that between a Creator and His Creature. The idea of an existence apart from and independent of God appears nowhere in scripture. God is the sole, unique, and absolute cause of all that exists. He has created all things by His Word and by His Spirit. There is no substance or principle of any kind to oppose Him; no material to tie Him down; no force to circumscribe His freedom.*

He speaks and things spring into being. He is the unrestricted owner of heaven and earth. There are no limits to His power; He does all that He sees fit to do. 'For Him and through Him and to Him are all things.' The world is the product of His will; it is the revelation of His perfections and finds its goal in His glory.[1]

Whether one is studying the ancient cultures of the Fertile Crescent, the various conquests of Europe, or events surrounding the discovery and settlement of the Americas, he must recognize that history finds its existence and relevance exclusively in God and His will for the universe. The whole of history is carried out in the theater of divine prerogative. As Cornelius Van Til stated:

All facts of history are what they are ultimately because of what God intends and makes them to be. Even that which is accomplished in human history through the instrumentality of men still happens by virtue of the plan of God. . . . He knows exhaustively because He controls completely.[2]

Therefore, for the Christian, the study of history can be defined as the inquiry into the relationship between God and His creation.

Any survey of world history is by its very nature a religious inquest. All men have an object of worship, and this basic core commitment influences their historical interpretation. They either worship and serve the Creator or the creation (Romans 1:25), and what they prioritize in their evaluation of history flows from this starting point. The study of history is thus an inescapably religious discipline.

Historians who embrace the skewed theory of evolution are every bit as religious as those historians who accept the biblical record of creation. The evolutionary philosophy of history is loosely supported atop a series of religious faith presuppositions, apart from which the whole system would collapse into ruin. R.J. Rushdoony explains:

When Darwin formulated his thesis, evolution was already a widely accepted concept. Going back to Hegel and his thinking, evolution had become accepted as the basic factor in all social thought. . . . Darwin did not go to nature, observe it, and then formulate his thesis, he went to contemporary philosophy, as well as to certain economic thinking, and derived his ideas of social evolution, and then applied these ideas to nature, and set about to prove that his already accepted hypothesis was true. Evolution is un-provable, it is a religious principle, and it is the basic religious premise of the modern world.[3]

In brief, Charles Darwin did not discover evolution; rather, he simply applied the already widely accepted social evolution of Hegel to the field of biology. This gave to the evolutionist what he had lacked up until that time: an object of faith in the material world, a religion of so-called science, and the introduction of the scientist as prophet.

Belief drives interpretation. How the historian discerns the ordinary from the extraordinary, the hero from the villain, or the timely from the timeless are all determined solely on the basis of his religious presuppositions—those core commitments he accepts by faith as the starting point of his worldview. The Christian historian presupposes that the framework for history is the divine act of creation, that man is unique to creation, that God is the uncontestable sovereign of the universe, that the many events in history are unified manifestations of a comprehensive plan of divine providence, and that every event in history finds it ultimate relevance in terms of divine covenant. The evolutionary historian, on the other hand, presupposes that the framework for history springs from chaos, that man is a mere animal of nature, that chaos is the only uncontestable certainty in the universe, that the many events in history are both random and meaningless, and that there is no ultimate relevance for any event in history. "The presuppositions of historians are therefore of the utmost importance," noted Rushdoony. "His learning may be massive, his scholarship ponderous, but the net result may be futile if his governing principle is a myth."[4]

In this lesson, Doug Phillips will lay the framework for a distinctly biblical philosophy of history and will explain why a diligent study of history is essential to the Christian world and life view. The most common myths and errors of modern historiography will be boldly confronted and vanquished, and a framework for a providential view of history will be firmly established in its place. At the conclusion of this lesson, the student who has mastered the material will be equipped to engage history with an understanding that every single event is the manifestation of God's comprehensive plan of providence. The student should also understand and be able to identify some of the major myths and errors involved in the modern study of history and be prepared to defend the biblical philosophy of history from Scripture.

LECTURE OUTLINE: 6000 YEARS OF EARTH HISTORY IN AN HOUR

I. **In the Beginning, God Created History (Gen. 1:1)**
    A. History is framed within the three dimensions of Creation
        1. Time
        2. Space
        3. Matter
    B. A Christian view of history is framed in the works of God's providence
    C. An evolutionary view of history is framed by chaos and is meaningless

II. **In the Beginning, God Prioritizes the Study of History (Gen. 1:14-19)**
    A. God created stars and lights to be for signs, seasons, days, and years
    B. The universe was created helio-centric, but is theologically geo-centric
    C. God's purpose for the cosmos reveals an implicit duty to study, record, and redeem history (Eph 5:15; Psalm 39:4; Psalm 90:12)

III. Our View of History is a Reflection of our Faith and Priorities

    A. Our commitment to the origin of history is reflected in either man's worship of God or worship of the creature (Rom. 1:22-25)

    B. History reflects infinite and cosmic personalism and meaning

    C. All men are inherently religious and interpret all facts through faith

    D. Jesus Christ is the central reference point for all of history

IV. The Study of History is More than a Study in Linear Time

    A. A study of history is a study of God's eternal decrees of providence

    B. God is sovereign over all things, and His historical decrees are certain

    C. The meaning and end of all history is directed to give glory to God alone

V. Seven Historical Myths that Must be Rejected

    A. The Myth of Uniformitarian Earth Chronology

    B. The Myth of the Corridor of Time

    C. The Myth of Racial Anthropology

    D. The Myth of Cultural Evolution

    E. The Myth of Cultural Equality

    F. The Myth of Glorious Paganism

    G. The Myth that the Present is the Key to the Past

VI. Christians Must Confront Four Errors Found in Modern Historiography

    A. The Conspiratorial View of History

    B. The Triumphalist View of History

    C. The Cynycist View of History

    D. The Cultural Relativist View of History

VII. The Providential Overview of Earth History Can be Divided Into 12 Cs

    A. The framework for all human conduct is established in Creation

    B. God unfolds the providential plan for His elect with a Commission

    C. War between mankind and Satan is introduced with the Fall and Curse

    D. Through patriarchy God preserves his people in the midst of Catastrophe

    E. As the world attempts to unite in apostasy at Babel, God puts them to Confusion

    F. The division of mankind into tribes, tongues, and nations develops various Cultures

    G. God establishes a people unto himself giving them a Law and Covenant

    H. A period of judgment and then preservation during a period of Captivity

    I. God takes on human flesh to redeem all creation in the life of Jesus Christ

    J. The reconciliation of all things to God is accomplished by Christ on the Cross

    K. Perseverance and reformation are accomplished by God through the Church

    L. Paradise is restored and the promises of God fulfilled at history's Consummation

VIII. Every Nation is a Theater in History that Illustrates the Tensions between Law and Liberty, Covenant and Idolatry, and Worship and Apostasy
  A. Evolution and statism attempt to unite the world against God
  B. God always preserves His people throughout history
  C. The Christian must pay close attention to the chronology of Scripture

IX. There are Five Reasons Why the Study of History is of Eternal Significance to the Christian
  A. Perseverance: We are to know God's providential history so that our sons and daughters will have hope in God in the day of adversity (Ps. 78)
  B. Perspective: We are to know God's providential history so that we will not judge the past by the present, but judge the present by the past
  C. Covenant: We are to know God's providential history worked out in the lives of flesh and blood men, so that we will be men of faith and be reminded to keep covenant with the God of our fathers
  D. Discipleship: Toledoth—when fathers proclaim the historic providence of God to their progeny, they fulfill the calling of generational discipleship (Is. 38:19; Deut. 32:7)
  E. Sanctification: We are to know the great providences of God in history so we can grow in love, appreciation, gratitude, and "boasting" for the God of our salvation

X. Our Prayers for You During This Course
  A. That you will use this as more than an opportunity for learning interesting facts
  B. That you will recognize that you are a steward of a limited piece of time
  C. That you will realize that you are an important part of history
  D. That you will realize that men fail and succeed in heroic service in similar ways
  E. That you will realize that you are God's representative to do His will in history
  F. That you will realize that secular history hides truth by redefining God and man
  G. That you will realize that those who control history define the culture

QUESTIONS

1. According to Genesis 1:1, how is the Christian view of time different from the evolutionary view of time?

2. How does our view of origins affect how we worship God?

3. What does Scripture say that God created in order to enable man to measure times and seasons?

4. All facts must be interpreted by faith assumptions called presuppositions. What is the Christian object by which all things are interpreted? What is the evolutionist object of faith?

5. How does Christianity answer the question of the "One and the Many"?

6. How is the Christian doctrine of providence important to the study of history?

7. Why is the biblical account of creation important to history?

8. How does the biblical view deal with the issue of racism? How does the Theory of Evolution perpetuate it?

9. Can any true meaning be given to life and the world apart from a biblical view of history?

10. How is Scripture to aid us in our study of history?

GROUP DISCUSSION/ASSIGNMENT

1. The ancient Greeks believed that their gods had authority over man, yet were subject to the forces of natural processes. The gods of Greece where believed to be products of nature themselves and subject to fatalism. By contrast, Scripture illustrates that God is not subject to time, space, or matter and cannot be manipulated by fate or the will of any other. Discuss the difference between the biblical doctrine of providence and the fatalism of Greek mythology. Also, contrast and discuss the implications of each of these positions when applied to a historical framework.

2. Early evolutionist William Hornaday made this statement: "One thing, however, is certain: The fence that marks the boundary between man and higher apes is neither so high nor so strong as that between the apes and the baboons. What I mean by this is that, excepting spoken language, the brightest apes are almost as intelligent and quite as handsome, as the lowest races of men."[5] Hornaday later followed his shameful hypothesis to its natural conclusion when he acquired Ota Benga, a slave from Congo, and in 1906 placed him on display at the New York Zoo with an orangutan. Discuss why the actions of William Hornaday are consistent with the evolutionary framework of history. Finally, discuss why a historian using the biblical framework of history will regard the actions of Mr. Hornaday as utterly reprehensible.

3. Evolutionist Julian Huxley summed up the basic religious pursuit of the modern age when he said, "Medieval theology urged men to think of human life in the light of eternity—*sub specie aeternitatis*: I am attempting to rethink it *sub specie evolutionis*—in the light of evolution."[6] Discuss why it is important for the Christian to think of all human life in terms of Scripture. Discuss also the clear antithesis presented in Huxley's statement.

4. It is critical to note that, just as there are many who have allowed evolution to masquerade as science, there are also those who claim to have a Christian worldview, yet who allow evolution to masquerade as biblical orthodoxy. In his book, *God and the Cosmos*, Dr. John Byl points out, "It is note worthy, however, that proponents of the literary [evolutionary] position often concede that, on purely exegetical grounds and excluding scientific evidence, the traditional interpretation is superior. [Bernard] Ramm, [Henric] Blocher, [Howard] Van Till, and [Davis] Young all explicitly state that their rejection of the literal reading of Genesis is primarily because of its presumed incompatibility with modern science." Ultimately, the

religious presuppositions of these individuals are not rooted in biblical faith, but rather in the mythology of modern science.[7] Consequently, the reproachful implications of such a faithless compromise are unavoidable. Discuss what the implications of such a compromise are. Also, discuss why it is important for the Christian historian to hold to the doctrine of the infallibility and sufficiency of Scripture.

5. In his book, *The Biblical Philosophy of History,* Dr. R.J. Rushdoony listed nine presuppositions of the biblical view of history that must be assumed by an individual who holds to the record of creation in Genesis 1.

    i.   The universe, time, history, man and all things are the handiwork of a sovereign, omnipotent, omniscient, and triune God

    ii. That history is to be understood primarily and essentially in terms of that God

    iii. That creation is described in Scripture as an act and history must be understood in terms of an act and not a process

    iv. That creation is totally under God's control

    v.   That time and history have meaning in terms of God's perfect and comprehensive plan

    vi. That the biblical philosophy of history is grounded on the doctrine of the infallibility of Scripture

    vii. That time is limited and does not issue from the primeval past, but from eternity

    viii. That man is active in nature but under the total authority of God

    ix. That God not only created the universe, but is personal and active in His relation to it; therefore, all facts in the universe are made personal to man

    Discuss why these presuppositions are antithetical to the evolutionary view of nature and history. Discuss also the implications of each with regard to how man is to view himself in light of creation in history.

6. According to biblical anthropology, man is created uniquely in the image of God. He is an active agent in the universe and has been commissioned by God to cultivate and take dominion of the earth. By contrast, according to evolutionary anthropology, man is a fairly young species on the earth and is evolved from nature. He is passive to the universe and is under the dominion of the brute factuality of nature. In short, man is nothing more than one random form among many. The guarantee of tomorrow is a desperate matter for the humanist. As a result, he will attempt to control history and nature by his own work of providence, or he will despair of history and nature. Contrast and discuss this with the biblical view that man is created unique in the image of God, and history and nature are the work of divine providence.

SCRIPTURE READINGS

Genesis 1-2

Isaiah 40:13-31

FURTHER READING

The Westminster Confession of Faith on God's Eternal Decree:

I. God from all eternity did by the most wise and holy counsel of his own will, freely and unchangeably ordain whatsoever comes to pass; yet so as thereby neither is God the author of sin; nor is violence offered to the will of the creatures, nor is the liberty or contingency of second causes taken away, but rather established.

II. Although God knows whatsoever may or can come to pass, upon all supposed conditions; yet hath he not decreed anything because he foresaw it as future, as that which would come to pass, upon such conditions.

III. By the decree of God, for the manifestation of his glory, some men and angels are predestinated unto everlasting life, and others foreordained to everlasting death.

IV. These angels and men, thus predestinated and foreordained, are particularly and unchangeably designed; and their number is so certain and definite that it cannot be either increased or diminished.

V. Those of mankind that are predestinated unto life, God, before the foundation of the world was laid, according to his eternal and immutable purpose, and the secret counsel and good pleasure of his will, hath chosen in Christ, unto everlasting glory, out of his free grace and love alone, without any foresight of faith or good works, or perseverance in either of them, or any other thing in the creature, as conditions, or causes moving him thereunto; and all to the praise of his glorious grace.

VI. As God hath appointed the elect unto glory, so hath he, by the eternal and most free purpose of his will, foreordained all the means thereunto. Wherefore they who are elected being fallen in Adam are redeemed by Christ, are effectually called unto faith in Christ by his Spirit working in due season; are justified, adopted, sanctified, and kept by his power through faith unto salvation. Neither are any other redeemed by Christ, effectually called, justified, adopted, sanctified, and saved, but the elect only.

VII. The rest of mankind, God was pleased, according to the unsearchable counsel of his own will, whereby he extendeth or withholdeth mercy as he pleaseth, for the glory of his sovereign power over his creatures, to pass by, and to ordain them to dishonor and wrath for their sin, to the praise of his glorious justice.

VIII. The doctrine of this high mystery of predestination is to be handled with special prudence and care that men attending to the will of God revealed in his Word and yielding obedience thereunto, may, from the certainty of their effectual vocation, be assured of their eternal election. So shall this doctrine afford matter of praise, reverence, and admiration of God; and of humility, diligence, and abundant consolation to all that sincerely obey the gospel.

SCRIPTURE MEMORY

Colossians 1:16-17, "For by him were all things created, that are in heaven, and that are in earth, visible and invisible, whether they be thrones, or dominions, or principalities, or powers: all things were created by him, and for him: And he is before all things, and by him all things consist."

Isaiah 46:9-11, "Remember the former things of old: for I am God, and there is none else; I am God, and there is none like me, Declaring the end from the beginning, and from ancient times the things that are not yet done, saying, My counsel shall stand, and I will do all my pleasure: Calling a ravenous bird from the east, the man that executeth my counsel from a far country: yea, I have spoken it, I will also bring it to pass; I have purposed it, I will also do it."

Psalm 39:4, "LORD, make me to know mine end, and the measure of my days, what it is: that I may know how frail I am."

John 1:3, "All things were made by him; and without him was not any thing made that was made."

DEFINITIONS

Antithesis: The rhetorical contrast of ideas by means of a contradictory antithesis asserted over against a thesis.

Cosmic Personalism: The faith assumption that every fact of the universe is by design, created exclusively by God and personal in relation to man.

Cosmic Impersonalism: The faith assumption that every fact of the universe is the product of random material forces in chaos one with another and are impersonal in relation to man.

Presupposition: The most basic faith assumptions in one's reasoning by which everything is interpreted and evaluated; the process by which opinions are formed.

Providence: The care and superintendence that God exercises over His creatures.

> *God the great Creator of all things does uphold, direct, dispose, and govern all creatures,*
> *actions, and things, from the greatest even to the least, by His most wise and holy providence,*
> *according to His infallible foreknowledge, and the free and immutable counsel of His*

own will, to the praise of the glory of His wisdom, power, justice, goodness, and mercy.
(Westminster Confession of Faith, Ch. V:1)

SUMMARY

For the Christian, the study of history is imperative because it ultimately involves the study of God and His relation to the universe. Equally important is the fact that our theology of the Scripture and creation is indispensable for providing the proper context, meaning, and true significance to every historical event in our world. History is not, as evolutionists suppose, the study of random events set within the framework of a universe dominated by brute facts and endless possibilities. Instead, the study of history is a theological inquiry into the providential work of God throughout the ages. Therefore, the chief cornerstone of any study of history is the sovereignty of God. He providentially orchestrates all things according to the good pleasure of His will. There is not one single object in the universe that has escaped his attention and total command. In essence, history cannot be known apart from the knowledge of God and His relation with the universe. A student who fails to acknowledge God at the center of his examination of history, fails to attain the true significance and reality of history. Consequently, such a person might be more properly considered a mythmaker rather than a true historian.

BIBLIOGRAPHY

Annals of the World, by Archbishop James Ussher

The Genesis Flood, by Dr. John Whitcomb and Dr. Henry Morris

The Biblical Philosophy of History, by Dr. R.J. Rushdoony

Back to Genesis, Conference Album (9 CDs) Vision Forum, Inc.

God and Cosmos: A Christian View of Time, Space, and the Universe, by John Byl

A Christian Survey of World History, by R.J. Rushdoony

END NOTES

1. Herman Bavinck, *Reformed Dogmatics, vol. 2, God and Creation* (Grand Rapids, MI: Baker Academic, 2006), p. 407.

2. Cornelius Van Til, *A Christian Theory of Knowledge* (Phillipsburg, NJ: Presbyterian and Reformed Publishing Co., 1969), p. 28.

3. R.J. Rushdoony, "The Closed Universe of Evolution," *Studies in Early Genesis*, Chalcedon Foundation, RR115(a)(i)

4. R.J. Rushdoony, *The Biblical Philosophy of History* (Phillipsburg, NJ: Presbyterian and Reformed Publishing Company, 1979), p. 11.

5. William T. Hornaday, "Three Great Apes," *Recreation VIII*, January-June 1898, p. 259.

6. Julian Huxley, *Evolution in Action* (New York: Penguin Group, 1963), p. 141.

7. John Byl, *God and Cosmos: A Christian View of Time, Space, and the Universe* (Carlisle, PA: Banner of Truth Trust, 2001), pp. 165-166.

NOTES

NOTES

CHAPTER 2

BIBLICAL CHRONOLOGY

INTRODUCTION

Little is known for certain about the world before the Great Flood outside of the record of Scripture. What, if anything, might be discovered through archeology is now buried under deep layers of flood strata. From the biblical record, however, there is a wealth of information that can be ascertained about this remarkable period of history. The time frame from the creation of the world up until the time of its judgment through the Global Deluge has been estimated to be around 1,655 years[1], comprising nearly one third of Earth's history. The opening four chapters in the book of Genesis are dedicated to shedding light on this astonishing era in world history which began in perfection and ended in global cataclysm.

The antediluvian period begins immediately after paradise was lost and our first parents experienced the expenditure of sweat, the pains of hunger, and the sentence of death for the first time in human existence. When Adam broke God's law in the Garden of Eden, the curse of death ensued. Adam died to God that day and with him all mankind. The most glorious circumstance of human life and liberty that has ever existed in the world was traded for mankind's death and total slavery to sin.

The world before the Flood was a world unlike any other. Mankind enjoyed a life expectancy which closely approached a millennium, as giants walked amid dinosaurs. The Scripture describes the antediluvian world as being a highly developed civilization in terms of knowledge and industry. Early on, for example, Cain and Abel are found to have had an operational knowledge of horticulture and animal husbandry. Later we are told that Cain built a city, a feat that required an extensive knowledge of such things as architecture, engineering, economics, and political science. We also learn that the earliest men were not restricted to the bare necessities of living, but made major advancements in the arts and sciences as well. The development of wind and string instruments, for instance, reflects a sophisticated knowledge of organology and musicology, while the development and working of brass and iron reflects an advanced understanding of metallurgy, chemistry, forging, and sculpture. The construction of the Ark alone reflects a vast body of knowledge that only a handful of civilizations have been able to boast since that time. While the dimensions of the Ark were divinely inspired, the knowledge, skill, and technology required for building such a vessel poses incredible challenges, even for modern cultures. While the antediluvian culture might be called ancient, it can in no way be accused of being primitive.

The Genesis record is rich with consternation for modern evolutionary anthropology and its false notion of cultural evolution. While evolutionists would have us believe that the first men were nomadic apes, wholly dependent on natural shelter, hunting and gathering, the Genesis record teaches that it was not until after the first cities were built that a nomadic style of living developed under the patriarchy of Jabal. Even so, these groups of families lived in tents, domesticated animals, and were engaged in a lucrative system of commerce. Consider also the fact that the antediluvian man had a life span more then ten times that of modern men. Moreover, he was not inhibited by any language barrier and was not subject to the intellectual and physical barriers caused by the millennia-long breakdown of human genes. Far from being "primitive", it becomes quite clear that the civilization of Noah's time could have been one of the most advanced civilizations ever to inhabit the earth.

It is during this time that we also find the establishment of some of the first forms of government. The family is the first and by far the most important of these. In fact, the family itself preceded the antediluvian age, and the greatest accomplishments of this period in history grew from the core of family industry. Accordingly, the decent of the age into widespread depravity is attributed chiefly to the corruption and dissolution of godly families. It is also important to note that God would preserve mankind from annihilation, not in terms of godly individuals, but rather in terms of a single godly family. The world that perished would rise and fall with the family—a pattern that has been perpetuated throughout the whole of world history.

It is also during this antediluvian period that we find the establishment of the church. In his commentary on Genesis 4:26 John Calvin observes, "We may readily conclude that Seth was an upright and faithful servant of God. And after he begat a son, like himself, and had a rightly constituted family, the face of the Church began distinctly to appear, and the worship of God was set up which might continue to posterity." Calvin goes on to remark on the similarity of this period with the Reformation. "Such a restoration of religion has been effected in our time; not that it had been altogether extinct; but there was no certainly defined people who called upon God; and, no sincere profession of faith, no uncorrupted religion could anywhere be established."[2] Indeed, it is historically noteworthy that the establishment of the church occurred as early as men began to multiply on the earth, and it has triumphantly persevered through even the most depraved period of time the world has ever known.

Furthermore, the Genesis record reveals that is was during this period that the first civilizations were established. Although the civil power to bear the sword to punish evildoers would not be expressly established by God until after the Flood (Gen. 9:6), we see at this time the establishment of cities and a division among men. However, any civil order that existed was quickly abandoned to such an extent that, in the days of Noah, we find a world steeped in rebellion and anarchy.

Yet the corruption of the old world did not occur overnight. It slowly took place over a period spanning well more than a millennium. Perhaps many might point to the failure of the church during this period. Indeed, it was a church given to apathy that was quick to assimilate to the godless culture surrounding it. Others may point to the virtual absence of the civil order and its inability to uphold righteousness and punish evil doers. Yet the specific cause of the universal moral corruption of the age is recorded in the sixth chapter of Genesis as being the near universal dissolution of the family. Specifically, the perpetuation of unequally yoked marriages between the "son of God" and the "daughters of men" was the devastating blow. The record shows that when children were born to them they were not trained up in the fear and admonition of the Lord, but rather became individuals renowned for wickedness. The disregard for the family was so widespread that, of the millions on the earth at the time, Noah was the only patriarch found to be perfect in his generations and righteous before the Lord.

Despite a multitude of historical landmarks and notable innovations, this era of world history has been justly overshadowed by the fact that it developed into the most wickedly decadent civilization ever to have inhabited the earth—a world of such pervasive malevolence, it invoked the Global Deluge and the annihilation of an estimated one billion inhabitants of the earth. We are told that "every imagination of the thoughts of [man's] heart was only evil continually" (Gen. 6:5); that in the final days of the old world, there was eating and drinking, marrying and giving in marriage, until the very hour the Flood came (Matt. 24:37-39). Though Noah was "a preacher of righteousness" (2 Peter 2:5), the wicked scoffed at his warnings, and "the world that then was, being overflowed with water, perished" (2 Peter 3:6).

This period of history is a sobering account of creation that fell under the dominion of man's unrestrained depravity. It illustrates the importance of maintaining integrity among the righteous, the significance of the family and the church to the whole of civilization, and God's unquenchable resolve to destroy the wicked and preserve a people for Himself.

In this lecture, Dr. John Whitcomb will survey this remarkable period of time from Creation to the Flood. Drawing from the Scripture and his years of experience, Dr. Whitcomb will explains the perfection of paradise lost, the depravity of the age to follow, and the applications that can be drawn from this period of time today. Dr. Whitcomb will discuss what it was like for the men who walked among the dinosaurs and came face to face with giants. In addition, the student will come to understand and appreciate the reliability of the biblical chronology over against the evolutionary theory of uniformitarianism.

LECTURE OUTLINE: BIBLICAL CHRONOLOGY

I.   God's Good Creation (Gen. 1:31)

    A.   Our first parents and all animals were exclusively herbivores

    B.   There was no death or shedding of blood in creation prior to man's fall

    C.   Throughout Creation Week, what God made was declared to be good but incomplete

    D.   God looked at His finished creation and declared that it was very good

    E.   There was perfect harmony and balance in the world God created

II.   Paradise Lost (Gen. 3)

    A.   The Fall of mankind is conjectured to have occurred shortly after creation

        1.   The forbidden tree was placed in the midst of the garden early in time

        2.   Eve had not become completely familiar with the animals in the Garden of Eden

        3.   Adam and Eve were commanded to multiply yet had no children prior to the Fall

    B.   Following the greatest age of the world was the worst age the world has known

III. The History of the World that Perished

    A.   At the time of the Deluge, the world population estimated at one billion people

    B.   There was a ruin of culture through unequally yoked marriages

    C.   The world was covered with corruption and violence

    D.   God pledged to not strive with man forever, but only for another 120 years

    E.   God destroyed a hopelessly depraved and unrepentant world

IV.   God Preserves the Righteous Amidst the Judgment

    A.   Noah was a man that was perfect in his generations

    B.   Noah was dependent on the grace of God as was any man

    C.   Noah was a light of righteousness among that corrupt and violent culture

V.   The World at that Time was Inhabited by Dinosaurs

    A.   The Bible provides an account of the origin, nature, and destiny of dinosaurs

    B.   Parents must discover and communicate the message of Genesis to their children

    C.   Job 40:15-24 tells us of a dinosaur called behemoth with remarkable features

D. Job 41:1-34 tells us of another dinosaur called leviathan that lived in the sea

E. The evolutionary chronology wrongly places dinosaurs seventy million years before man appeared, yet Job was an eyewitness to these remarkable creatures

F. Evolutionary uniformitarianism wrongly places the last dinosaurs seventy million years before man

G. Christians must reject the unsupportable myths of evolution and turn their hearts and faith to the Scriptures for truth

H. All sea creatures were created on the fifth day of Creation, including those now extinct such as dinosaurs

VI. God Provided for the Preservation of Life on the Earth

A. Noah and his family were the only humans to survive

B. Every kind of fowl in the air was preserved in the Ark

C. Every kind of land animal, including dinosaurs, was preserved in the Ark

D. The Ark had a capacity of 1,396,000 cubic feet

E. The Ark was so large that two of every animal today could fit in just one of the three decks

F. This means that up to two-thirds of the animals that existed at that time are now extinct

G. Dinosaurs never stopped growing, so it is likely the young were brought onto the Ark to represent their kinds

H. The Flood provided a massive fossil record found all over the earth

I. The dinosaurs, along with a host of other animals, are now an example that the earth is not evolving, but rather it is dying out

VII. Conclusion

A. The initial extent of the curse was unbearable, but through Noah, God brought comfort

B. God has brought relief to our world through the washing away of the Old World that perished

QUESTIONS

1. Prior to the Fall of man and the subsequent curse, what did the dinosaurs eat?

2. What are the affects of unequally yoked marriages on the rest of society?

3. How many years was the Old World given to repent?

4. What does it mean that Noah was perfect in his generations?

5. Are there examples of dinosaurs mentioned in the Scriptures? Where?

6. Where did the dinosaurs come from?

7. How does animal extinction lend support for the testimony of Scripture over against evolution?

8. How does the fossil record testify of the biblical chronology of earth history?

9. Why is it important for parents to study the Genesis record and teach it to their children?

10. How was God's judgment of the wicked a demonstration of God's grace on men living today?

GROUP DISCUSSION/ASSIGNMENT

1. From the testimony of Scripture, we are provided with an account of the last days of the Old World leading up to the Global Deluge. We are told that, in days preceding the Flood, the world was eating and drinking, marrying and giving in marriage, and knew nothing until the waters came and carried them all away. Even as those in these last days scoff at the historicity of the Flood and the coming judgment, those who lived before the Global Deluge scoffed at God's judgment and likely shared the sentiment described in II Peter 3:4, "Where is the promise of His coming? . . . [for] all things continue as they were from the beginning of creation." Albert Einstein wrote, "I cannot conceive of a God who rewards and punishes his creatures, or has a will of the type of which we are conscious in ourselves. . . . In their struggle for the ethical good, teachers of religion must have the stature to give up a personal God, that is, give up that source of fear and hope which in the past placed such vast power in the hands of priests. . . ."[3] Discuss similarities of this statement made by Dr. Einstein with the scoffing of the world that perished, as well as the similarities of the inevitable outcome.

2. There are essentially three views as to the identity of the "sons of God" and the "daughters of men", as recorded in Genesis 6. The first view is one held among orthodox rabbinical Judaism which has been adopted by only a few Christian expositors. According to this view, the sons of God are identified as the sons of earthly nobles, while the daughters of men are identified as women from lower orders in society. This interpretation relies on the latter part of verse four, "and they bare children to them, the same became mighty men which were of old, men of renown." This view has been widely disregarded as being unsupported by the text. A second more popular view identifies the sons of God as a multitude of fallen angels. The daughters of men are identified as human women. Proponents of this viewpoint make the case that the "sons of God" mentioned in passages such as Job 1:6; 2:1; 38:7 and Daniel 3:25 are unquestionably angels. Those who hold to this position also appeal to such texts in 2 Peter 2:4-6 and Jude 6 which mention the judgment of angels. However, the third view is by far the most widely accepted among Christian commentators. The sons of God are identified as the male descendents of Seth who called upon the name of the Lord. The daughters of men are identified as the female descendents of Cain. Commentators who hold to this view point out that the righteous are called the sons of God in Hosea 1:10 and Psalm 80:17. This view heavily emphasizes the familial distinction developed in the fourth and fifth chapters of Genesis between the righteous line of Seth and the vagabond line of Cain. Discuss these three views as well as some of the historical and theological implications of each.

3. Dr. Donald Chittick states the following with regard to the Antediluvian Age, "If people had already advanced this far so early in their development of civilization, organized agriculture, musical instruments, and metallurgy, what could have developed in the many remaining years before Noah's Flood? May I suggest for consideration that, by the time of Noah's Flood, they may well have developed a level of science and technology that we haven't matched until the twentieth century or even possibly that we may not yet have attained."[4] Compare and discuss this in light of the evolutionary notion of cultural evolution.

4. The Flood was the supreme demonstration of God's resolution to redeem the earth from the curse, and the account was never forgotten in the ancient world. There is estimated to be over 270 floods account from various cultures all over the world. Throughout biblical prophecy, there are references to seas and waters which are invoked to stress that God is not slack in his determination to judge the wicked and protect the righteous (Is. 28:2, 17; Ezek. 13:11-13, 27:34; Hab. 3:9-10). Discuss the significance of this theme in light of the event spoken of in Matthew 8:23-27 and the impact it must have had on the disciples of Christ. Also discuss this theme in light of Rev. 21:1 which indicates that in the new heavens and earth there will be no sea.

5. In his book, *The Waters Above*, Dr. Joseph C. Dillow describes the devastating implications of a Global Flood: "Without a doubt the collapse by condensation of such a vast vapor canopy would result in untold devastation and deluge all over the planet. For forty feet of water to pour from the heavens over all the earth for a period of forty days and nights (0.5 inches per hour) would unleash a fantastic flood catastrophe. The swollen rivers would wash sediments into the oceans. Sedimentation would be rapid as billions of tons of sediments were carried by the raging flood waters and redeposited. Volcanic activity and earthquakes would have lead to the uplift of continents, tidal waves, and the formation of the mountain ranges."[5] Discuss the implications of a worldwide flood as it relates to the evolutionary doctrine of uniformitarian earth chronology.

6. The deception of the Serpent is the very same deception mankind must defend against today. "Ye shall be as gods," said the Serpent, "knowing good and evil." In mankind's original state prior to the Fall, he had a free will and knowledge of what was right and wrong. For instance, Eve recited the commandment of God to the serpent (though she added to it regarding the issue of touching the fruit), "We may eat of the fruit of the trees of the garden: But of the fruit of the tree which is in the midst of the garden, God hath said, 'Ye shall not eat of it, neither shall ye touch it, lest ye die.'" (Genesis 3:2-3) Mankind knew God as the only Lawgiver, and that right and wrong were determined by Him alone. However, Satan tempted mankind with the notion that they would be as gods, determining for themselves what was right and wrong without reference to God. Discuss the implications and ultimate consequences of man's determining for himself what is right and wrong as it pertains to the antediluvian civilization. Also discuss how this same satanic lie is perpetuated in modern thinking.

SCRIPTURE READINGS

2 Peter 2

Job 12:7-22

Isaiah 45:18-25

FURTHER READING

A Selection from Thomas Goodwin's comments on 1 Peter 3:19-21, "How the story of Noah was a type of the Mediator of the covenant of grace, Christ which was the Ark."[6]

But when I came upon this occasion narrowly to examine this matter,

1. I considered that the salvation by waters of the flood held not at all a correspondence with our salvation, through our being washed in Christ's blood, as in baptism is signified; whereas here the apostle affirms, that there is a like figure answering each other, which, to be sure, holds not in this. For the persons of those in the ark were not washed by the water of the flood at all, as we are washed in baptism by Christ's blood; but it was the ark only which was washed with those waters.

2. I found that the salvation of Noah is said to have been in and by the ark. So expressly in the text, 'wherein (speaking of the ark) 'eight personas were saved' as the means of their salvation; and as for the waters saving them, that was but an accidental effect, for otherwise the waters overflowing tended to destroy them.

3. I found that *dia hydor* translated here '*by* the water' is more properly, both to the sense and phrase, rendered '*through* the water,' and so the sense is; in the ark they were saved from the flood, being carried in it through all its waves, and still kept safe from all danger from them; as in the Acts. Chap. iv. 22, it is through many tribulations that we enter into glory (it is the same principle). So these were saved through these waters which otherwise of themselves, directly and indeed, did threaten and hazard their salvation. Again I found *dia hydor* is rendered in this very epistle, 'in the water,' or in the midst of the water, by this very apostle that kept to his own dialect: 2 Epist. iii. 5, 'The earth that now stands in the water,' or, 'in the midst of the water.' Just thus here, they were saved in the ark, floating in or through the midst of the waters.

4. So as those words, *the like figure whereunto*, refer not, 1, to the word *water*, but unto the word ark as 'wherein' it is said, 'they were saved;' 2, or else, unto the matter of that whole foregoing sentence, and so the coherence runs thus, that the substance of our salvation by baptism, or Christian baptism, answers in similitude unto that salvation to those eight persons in the ark then, and is a like figure thereunto.

The summary of all is that Christ our ark, and our salvation in him, now signified in baptism, was the thing lively forefigured in that salvation of theirs in the ark, bearing them up in and through the waters.

SCRIPTURE MEMORY

John 5:39-47, "Search the scriptures; for in them ye think ye have eternal life: and they are they which testify of me. And ye will not come to me, that ye might have life. I receive not honour from men. But I know you, that ye have not the love of God in you. I am come in my Father's name, and ye receive me not: if another shall come in his own name, him ye will receive. How can ye believe, which receive honour one of another, and seek not the honour that cometh from God only? Do not think that I will accuse you to the Father: there is one that accuseth you, even Moses, in whom ye trust. For had ye believed Moses, ye would have believed me; for he wrote of me. But if ye believe not his writings, how shall ye believe my words?"

2 Cor. 5:10, "For we must all appear before the judgment seat of Christ; that every one may receive the things done in his body, according to that he hath done, whether it be good or bad."

1 Peter 3:20, "Which sometime were disobedient, when once the longsuffering of God waited in the days of Noah, while the ark was a preparing, wherein few, that is, eight souls were saved by water."

DEFINITIONS

Antediluvian: That period of time which began directly after the Fall and ended with the Global Flood

Catastrophism: A view that holds that the earth has periodically been subject to sudden cataclysmic events which have altered its characteristics over time

Chronology: The science that deals with measuring time by regular divisions and that assigns to events their proper dates

Nephilim: A race of giant men who lived on the earth prior to the Flood

Uniformitarianism: An evolutionary theory which assumes that the same natural processes that operate in the universe have always operated in the same manner as we observe them presently

SUMMARY

The evolutionary theory of uniformitarian chronology has led evolutionists to view the present world as a key to the past. Moreover, the evolutionary theory of cultural evolution paints modern man as far superior to civilizations of the past. In effect, the evolutionary view of history is at its very root a rejection of history in favor of the modern world and modern man. If the evolutionist must invent billions of years to support the myth of uniformitarian chronology and make apes out of men to support the myth of cultural evolution, he will do so in spite of history in order to support his modern assumptions. Yet, if we believe the Scripture, we can expect that the mythology of the modern evolutionist will eventually go the way of the Greco-Roman mythologies of old.

Yet, for the Christian, history is more than the study of linear time. It is the study of the character of God and His eternal prerogative as it is carried out through time and space in history. In fact, we are commanded in Scripture to "remember the days of old, consider the years of many generations" (Deuteronomy 32:7). Consequently, it is essential that the historian have a biblical view of chronology. The account of Noah's Flood and the world that perished stands in direct opposition to the myths of uniformitarian chronology and cultural evolution. Not only does it provide a record of a global catastrophe which drastically reshaped the physical structure of the earth, but it also provides an account of the earliest civilizations as being highly advanced and in no way "primitive". In summary, the Christian historian must emphatically insist on a consistently biblical view of earth chronology and cultural development.

BIBLIOGRAPHY

The Genesis Flood, by Dr. John Whitcomb and Dr. Henry Morris

The World that Perished, by Dr. John Whitcomb

The Puzzle of Ancient Man, by Dr. Donald E. Chittick

To Be As Gods, by Dr. R.J. Rushdoony.

Evolution: The Fossils Still Say No!, by Dr. Duane Gish

END NOTES

1. James Ussher, *Annals of World History* (Green Forest, AR: Master Books, Inc.), p. 19.

2. John Calvin, *Calvin's Commentaries*, Vol. I, Book of Genesis (Ada, MI: Baker Books, 1974), p. 224.

3. Albert Einstein, as quoted in John Byl, *The Divine Challenge: On Matter, Mind, Math & Meaning* (Carlisle, PA: Banner of Truth, 2004), p. 1.

4. Donald E. Chittick, *The Puzzle of Ancient Man* (Newberg, OR: 1998), pp. 37-38.

5. Joseph C. Dillow, *The Waters Above* (Chicago, IL: Moody Publishers, 1982), p. 183.

6. Thomas Goodwin, *The Works of Thomas Goodwin, vol. IX* (Edinburgh: James Nichol, 1864), p. 83.

NOTES

CHAPTER 3

GOD THE RULER OF ALL NATIONS

INTRODUCTION

The traveler who passes through the land is at first inclined to say that there are no ruins, no remains, of the mighty city which once lorded over the earth, though there are no arches, no pillars, but one or two appearances of masonry even—yet the whole country is covered with traces of exactly the kind which it was prophesied Babylon should leave. Vast "heaps" or mounds, shapeless and unsightly, are scattered at intervals over the entire region where it is certain that Babylon anciently stood.[1] —George Rawlinson

The city and tower of Babylon were built to perpetuate the old Edenic conspiracy: that men should be as gods, determining for themselves what is good and evil.[2] It was there that men would be united together in idolatry and tyranny. This is indicated in the tenth chapter of the book of Genesis: "And they said, Go to, let us build us a city and a tower, whose top may reach unto heaven; and let us make us a name, lest we be scattered abroad upon the face of the whole earth" (Genesis 11:4). Herein lies the objective and motive of early Babylon.

The city and the tower were their object. The city was to be the seat of civil power, and the tower was to be the seat of worship. The tower proposed was a ziggurat, a large-stepped pyramid complete with a temple built onto its summit. The motives of these early social engineers are revealing. The tower itself was not intended to physically reach heaven, but rather it was meant to unite the people in an idolatrous religious cult and thus rival Heaven. The second motivation was to establish for themselves positions of power and authority as Dr. R.J. Rushdoony explains:

> Then the plan was this: "let us make us a name" (v. 4), or, a shem, meaning let us define ourselves, fix and establish our authority so that we are what we declare ourselves to be. Instead of being defined by the image of God (Gen. 1:26-28), man now held that he would be his own creature and creation and would define himself. If man becomes a self-definer, he then, like a god, names and defines everything else.[3]

Thus, Babel was established to be a world order which would unify mankind against God under global idolatry and tyranny. If successful, the Lord said, nothing would have been restrained from them which they had imagined to do. And so the Lord confounded the languages so that the hope to universally indoctrinate mankind with a worldview of tyranny and idolatry became instantly unattainable.

Those who remained in the city would strive to realize this goal. The tower of Babel would be destroyed and rebuilt several times leading up to its final restoration during the reign of Nebuchadnezzar. Babylon would become a "holy city" of the ancient world and would later become the dominant civil power in the world. Yet, at the time that it seemed Babylon would finally reach its lofty ambitions, the prophet Isaiah heralded that the city's long tradition of tyranny and idolatry would soon come to an end:

> Babylon, the glory of kingdoms, the beauty of the Chaldees' excellency, shall be as when God overthrew Sodom and Gomorrah. It shall never be inhabited, neither shall it be dwelt in from generation to generation: neither shall the Arabian pitch tent there; neither shall the shepherds make their fold there. . . . and her time is near to come, and her days shall not be prolonged.[4]

And so, as with all of mankind's utopian conspiracies, the pride of Babylonia would inevitably find its resting place beneath a remote desert floor.

Babylon, however, would not be survived long by the monarchy of Judea. Israel had become a society steeped in what Scripture characterizes as flagrant idolatry; what we might characterize today as religious pluralism. Even as the children of Israel adopted new gods and co-mingled the worship of Jehovah with the worship of pagan deities, they still believed that the God of their fathers would preserve Jerusalem, as it was the seat of the house of David, the location of His temple, and the chief city of His covenant people.[5] God had sent prophets to call the nation to repentance and to warn of His approaching judgment. Yet Israel refused to heed the teachings of those men of God. Instead they would satisfy themselves with the prophets who "healed the hurt . . ., saying, 'Peace, peace; when there [was] no peace.'"[6]

The idolatry of God's people is essential for understanding the purpose for which God had raised up Babylon. The Chaldeans, as the Babylonians were called, were ordained as an instrument of judgment against the northern kingdom of Judah:

> *Behold ye among the heathen, and regard, and wonder marvelously: for I will work a work in your days which ye will not believe, though it be told you. For, lo, I raise up the Chaldeans, that bitter and hasty nation, which shall march through the breadth of the land, to possess the dwelling places that are not theirs. . . . They shall come all for violence: their faces shall sup up as the east wind, and they shall gather the captivity as the sand.*[7]

The Scripture makes plain that God alone rises up nations and puts them down again according to His purpose. The golden age of Babylon was no exception. Though Babylon was a vessel of dishonor, it had been raised up and directed according to God's divine purpose.[8]

In this lecture, Dr. Paul Jehle will walk students through the history of Babylon from its founding under Cush to the day God wrote its doom on the palace wall before King Belshazzar. Dr. Jehle will also outline the deeply satanic roots of the Babylonian kingdom and how the legacy of this ancient empire influences the world today. Babylon is an historic example of the antithesis between pride and humility. The satanic legacy that lies at the root of both idolatry and tyranny will be revealed, and ultimately it will be shown that, despite what we may perceive as the triumph of darkness in history, God uses vessels of dishonor to accomplish His perfect plan for the good of those who are call according to His purpose.

LECTURE OUTLINE: BABYLON — PRIDE AND HUMILITY

I.   **Pride Versus Humility (Proverbs 16:19; Daniel 4:37)**

II.   **Liberty throughout History**
    A.   Ancient History: Law without Liberty
    B.   Middle History: Christ—The Law of Liberty
    C.   Modern History: Liberty without Law

III. **The Second Millennium: "The Development of Nations"**
    A.   Founded by Cush, son of Ham and father of Nimrod
    B.   The Babylon Empire, the root of all pagan religions
        1.   Babel; Belus; Baal; "god of confusion"
        2.   The Goddess Mother and the Son are symbolized in pagan religions
        3.   Demonic gods demanding blood sacrifice and sexual perversion
    C.   The Tower of Babel and the Dispersion (2150 BC)

D. Babylon in the Bible: A Symbol of Pride, Rebellion, and Witchcraft

E. The Fear of the Lord: Key to Humility and Honor

IV. The Fourth Thousand Years: "The Captivity of God's People"

A. Assyrian Empire (power)

B. Babylonian Empire (pride)

C. A Persian Empire (The Law of the Medes and Persians)

D. Greek Empire (pleasure)

V. The New Babylonian Empire: "A Revival of Pride and Rebellion"

A. New Babylon rules the earth for 88 years (606-538 BC)

B. Nabopolassar was co-ruler with his son until 606 BC

C. Nebuchadnezzar reigned for half the dynasty (44 years)

    1. A "divine" monarch who built fortification walls 87 x 350 feet

    2. Erected hanging gardens for his wife to be like her homeland

    3. Took conquered people as captives for slave labor

    4. Emulated the pride of Babylon

    5. Humbled by God, his wife ruled in his place

    6. Repented before the Lord

VI. Israel under the Yoke of an "An Empire of Pride"

A. Josiah's revival and reforms (636 BC-609 BC)

B. Generational continuity between Josiah, Jeremiah, and Daniel

C. Jeremiah warns of 70 years of captivity (609 BC)

D. Daniel taken captive at the age of sixteen (609 BC)

E. Daniel interprets the king's dream (605 BC)

F. Shadrach, Meshach, Abednego refuse idolatry (595 BC)

G. Judah taken captive (586 BC)

H. Nebuchadnezzar humbled (570-563 BC)

I. Nebuchadnezzar dies after his conversion (562 BC)

J. Daniel interprets the handwriting on the wall (539 BC)

K. Daniel in the lion's den (539 BC)

L. Decree of Cyrus for Jews to return (538 BC)

VII. Lessons from Daniel: "How to Conquer Pride"

A. Believers must embrace a kingdom understanding

B. Believers must be willing to embrace a philosophy of separation

C. Believers must learn to minister in captivity through love and service

D. Believers must embrace the cross and not promote themselves

E. "Overcome evil with good" (Romans 12:21)

QUESTIONS

1. What three relationships between law and liberty have been perpetuated throughout history?

2. Where does the religious symbol of the mother and child originate?

3. Where does Scripture tell us that languages come from and why?

4. How is satanic worship reflected in Babylonian art?

5. What is the name "Babylon" used to signify today?

6. What does the conversion of Nebuchadnezzar teach us about evangelism?

7. How old was the prophet Jeremiah when his prophecies began to be recorded?

8. What does Nebuchadnezzar teach us about how God responds to pride?

9. How do Josiah, Jeremiah, and Daniel present a pattern of multigenerational continuity?

10. What was one of the political policies Daniel made as prime minister which was also greatly reflected in early American political thought?

GROUP DISCUSSION/ASSIGNMENT

1. God used Babylon to carry the Jews out of the land and scatter them throughout the earth. Many of them would return to Judah and rebuild, but the majority would remain in the lands where they had been scattered. Some of the exiles repented of their idolatry and built the first synagogues. The synagogues must have seemed rather humble to those Jews who remembered the glory of the temple. Yet, by the time Christ had come, there existed an extensive network of synagogues throughout the entire world, through which apostolic Christianity would be able to carry the gospel to every nation. The destruction of Jerusalem at the hands of the Babylonians may have seemed like the final triumph of darkness to those Hebrew contemporaries, yet for the Christian, the judgment of God was also a providential staging point through which all nations would be blessed with the light of the Gospel.

   Discuss this fact in light of the attitude of many Christians in our modern day who believe that we are witnessing the final triumph of darkness. Could the evil that we are witnessing be the judgment of God for the idolatry and complacency so common among modern churches? How might the present age be a staging point for bringing glory to God in future generations?

2. There are an estimated 6,912 languages in the world today, which break down into 94 separate, distinct, and unrelated language families. If we measure the rate of change which takes place in language today, we find that the time that it should take for 6,912 languages to develop from 94 families is around four thousand years. Discuss why this fact is devastating to the evolutionist who supposes that all languages can be traced back to a single language.

3. Dr. Cornelius Van Til once stated that "Even that which is accomplished in human history

through the instrumentality of men still happens by virtue of the plan of God."[9] In contrast, a conspiratorial view of history holds that history is dominated by human conspiracies. Thus, the conspiratorialist is always looking for a few powerful individuals or groups who secretly impose their wills on world history. Discuss what the story of Babylon teaches us about the inevitable fate of all human conspiracies and the true nature of human conspiracies in light of God's providence.

4. Genesis 10:8-9 introduces Nimrod whose name literally means "we will revolt." The Scripture describes him as becoming a mighty one on the earth. This phrase is used in the same sense as it is used for the antedeluvians in Genesis 6:4. We are also told that Nimrod was "the mighty hunter before the LORD." As Keil and Delitzsch have it in their commentary on Genesis:

    Nimrod was mighty in hunting, and that in opposition to Jehovah; not before Jehovah in the sense of, according to the purpose and will of Jehovah. . . . In addition to this, Nimrod as a mighty hunter founded a powerful kingdom; and the founding of this kingdom is shown by the verb. . . . Hence, if the expression "a mighty hunter" relates primarily to hunting in the literal sense, we must add to the literal meaning the figurative signification of a 'hunter of men'. . . . This course of life gave occasion to the proverb, "like Nimrod, a mighty hunter against the Lord," which immortalized not his skill in hunting beasts, but the success of his hunting of men in the establishment of an imperial kingdom by tyranny and power.

    Contrast and discuss the description of Nimrod as being a "mighty hunter of men" with the statement made by Christ to his disciples in Mark 1:17, "Come ye after me, and I will make you to become fishers of men."

5. Pyramids have been built in diverse places by various civilizations all over the world, all of which are connected with idolatrous worship. This is evidence that though the people were divided and dispersed at Babel, many groups settled in their respective places and built their own towers to perpetuate that original quest for idolatry and tyranny. Discuss whether or not modern civilization has given up that quest, and though we are not building pyramids, what other means are used to unite people under a system of idolatry and tyranny.

SCRIPTURE READINGS

Genesis 10-11

Daniel 4

FURTHER READING

Institutes of the Christian Religion: What is it to know God

By the knowledge of God, I understand that by which we not only conceive that there is some God, but also apprehend what it is for our interest, and conducive to his glory, what, in short, it is befitting to know concerning him. For, properly speaking, we cannot say that God is known where there is no religion or piety. I am not now referring to that species of knowledge by which men, in themselves lost and under curse, apprehend God as a Redeemer in Christ the Mediator. I speak only of that simple and primitive knowledge, to which the mere course of nature would have conducted us, had Adam stood upright. For although no man will now, in the present ruin of the human race, perceive God to be either a father, or the author of salvation, or propitious in any respect, until Christ interpose to make our peace; still it is one thing to perceive that God our Maker supports us by his power, rules us by his providence, fosters us by his goodness, and visits us with all kinds of blessings, and another thing to embrace the grace of reconciliation offered to us in Christ. Since, then, the Lord first appears, as well in the creation of the world as in the general doctrine of Scripture, simply as a Creator, and afterwards as a Redeemer in Christ,—a twofold knowledge of him hence arises: of these the former is now to be considered, the latter will afterwards follow in its order.

But although our mind cannot conceive of God, without rendering some worship to him, it will not, however, be sufficient simply to hold that he is the only being whom all ought to worship and adore, unless we are also persuaded that he is the fountain of all goodness, and that we must seek everything in him, and in none but him. My meaning is: we must be persuaded not only that as he once formed the world, so he sustains it by his boundless power, governs it by his wisdom, preserves it by his goodness, in particular, rules the human race with justice and judgement, bears with them in mercy, shields them by his protection; but also that not a particle of light, or wisdom, or justice, or power, or rectitude, or genuine truth, will anywhere be found, which does not flow from him, and of which he is not the cause; in this way we must learn to expect and ask all things from him, and thankfully ascribe to him whatever we receive. For this sense of the divine perfections is the proper master to teach us piety, out of which religion springs. By piety I mean that union of reverence and love to God which the knowledge of his benefits inspires. For, until men feel that they owe everything to God, that they are cherished by his paternal care, and that he is the author of all their blessings, so that nought is to be looked for away from him, they will never submit to him in voluntary obedience; nay, unless they place their entire happiness in him, they will never yield up their whole selves to him in truth and sincerity.[10]

SCRIPTURE MEMORY

Proverbs 18:12, "Before destruction the heart of man is haughty, and before honor is humility."

1 Peter 5:5-6, "Likewise, ye younger, submit yourselves unto the elder. Yea, all of you be subject one to another, and be clothed with humility: for God resisteth the proud, and giveth grace to the humble. Humble yourselves therefore under the mighty hand of God, that he may exalt you in due time:"

Romans 12:1-2, "I beseech you therefore, brethren, by the mercies of God, that ye present your bodies a living sacrifice, holy, acceptable unto God, which is your reasonable service. And be not conformed to this world: but be ye transformed by the renewing of your mind, that ye may prove what is that good, and acceptable, and perfect, will of God."

DEFINITIONS

Conspiratorial View of History: A theory of history which holds that all or most historical events can be explained in terms of human conspiracies, so that the conspiratorialist is always looking for small elites who secretly govern the affairs of world history.

Multigenerational Continuity: The process by which the teaching and ideas of one generation is transferred to another generation and faithfully preserved.

Pluralism: A false belief system that holds that there are several varieties of ultimate reality which coexist at the same time. For instance, religious pluralism is a modern day form of polytheism (the belief in two or more gods).

Tyranny: The encroachment on another's life, liberty, or property by power without authority.

SUMMARY

Babylon began its history with a short-lived conspiracy where men sought to reject God as the author of life and history and instead attempted to shape history according to their own wills. From that time, this pattern has become a well-established rule throughout history: that where there is tyranny, it will be found to be inseparably coupled with idolatry. The legacy of Babylonian thought survived and has been adopted by a multitude of nations and incorporated into ideologies that seek to unite the world under one tyrannical and idolatrous banner. Yet the history of Babylon teaches the utter futility of human conspiracies. God alone is sovereign over all the universe; He rules the nations. He alone directs the ascent of kings and the rise and fall of empires. In fact, the more rebellious a people become, the tighter they fit a noose around their own neck. The Christian historian must view all events in history as the handiwork of God and understand them in light of God's plan of redemption. The Christian need not fear if it appears that tyranny and idolatry cannot be overthrown in the present evil age. Babylon teaches us that the end of even the most prominent in the world can be brought about by God in the space of only an hour.

BIBLIOGRAPHY

Israel and the Nations, by F.F. Bruce

Handwriting on the Wall, by James B. Jordan

The Sacred and Profane History of the World, by Samuel Shuckford

Ruler of Nations, by Gary DeMar

END NOTES

1. George Rawlinson, *The Five Great Monarchies of the Ancient World*, vol. 2, *The Second Monarchy*, (London: William Clowes & Sons, 1871), p. 520.

2. Genesis 3:5.

3. R.J. Rushdoony, *Commentaries on the Pentateuch, Vol. I, Commentary on Genesis* (Vallecito, CA: Ross House Books, 2004), p. 110.

4. Isaiah 13:19-22.

5. F.F. Bruce, *Israel and the Nations* (Grand Rapids, MI: Wm. B. Eerdmans Publishing Company, 1963), p. 85.

6. Jeremiah 8:11.

7. Habakkuk 1:5-9.

8. Romans 9:13-23.

9. Cornelius Van Til, *A Christian Theory of Knowledge*, (Phillipsburg, NJ: Presbyterian & Reformed, 1969), p. 28.

10. John Calvin, *Institutes of the Christian Religion*, Trans. Henry Beveridge (Grand Rapids, MI: Wm. B. Eerdmans Publishing Company, 1953), Bk. I, ch. II, sec. I.

NOTES

NOTES

CHAPTER 4

CHRISTIANITY AND CULTURE

INTRODUCTION

As the first generation of faithful American patriots and statesmen passed away, American culture began to take a fatal turn toward Hellenization and the myth of glorious paganism. One contemporary poet of that period captured the spirit of that age well when he observed, "Thy Naiad airs have brought me home, to the glory that was Greece and the grandeur that was Rome."[1] But what was the so-called "glory" and "grandeur" of Greece and Rome? The late Otto Scott answered the question this way:

> That 'grandeur' was based on slavery, and used torture as an instrument of the courts, and human sacrifice as part of religion and politics. . . . Virtually all "classical" scholars shrink from describing the lack of individual rights under paganism, and are remarkably silent about paganism's human sacrifices. . . . Euripides described the Greek sacrifice of Iphigenia; Herodotus described the human sacrifice in Egypt, Plato spoke of human sacrifices as "a common custom."[2]

The Greek civilization was built on the backs of slaves who at times outnumbered freemen by as much as five to one. Human sacrifice was commonplace not only in religious worship, but in political ceremonies on occasion as well. Sexual perversion of every kind was not only routine, but it was also seen as virtuous, so that women and children received no protection from the debauchery of Greek men. Individual liberty was non-existent as man was seen as a social animal whose claim to rights, if any, were completely at the mercy of the state. In many places, it was illegal to allow a child with disabilities to live, and abortion was not only officially authorized, but, in some cases, it was mandatory. It is in Greece that we discover the development of some of the first compulsory education laws, as children were considered children of the state rather than of their parents. It is this form of paganism that many have sought to resurrect and glorify in modern culture.

Dr. Henry Van Til pointed out that "culture is religion externalized."[3] These characteristics of Greek culture, therefore, are not random attributes collectively woven together. Rather, they are consistent manifestations of the Greco-Roman religious presuppositions. The cultural themes and ideas reflected in the laws, attitudes, education, philosophy, and art of a nation are all birthed from the common womb of the predominate religion of that nation. It is in this sense that the Greek culture provides an antithesis to the culture of biblical Christianity, and this antithesis points to the greater battle for civilization.

The primary theme that lies between Greek and Hebrew culture is the distinction between God the Creator and man the creature. According to the Scripture, man is made in the image of God. Due to his sin nature, he is fallen and therefore is nothing apart from some measure of grace from God. According to the Greek, by contrast, man is the measure of all things, and his mind is capable of discovering all truth without reference to the grace of God. The gods, the Greeks argue, were made in the image of man and subject to like passions.

Scripture tells us that God is the absolute sovereign over every aspect of the universe, and that goodness and virtue are determined by the law of God. The ancient Greeks, by contrast, maintained that the State is the ultimate authority over man; man is a creature of the state, and goodness and virtue are determined by his service to the state. Therefore, these two opposing religious presuppositions which have dominated Western culture for two thousand years can be reduced to a single theme: sovereignty. The question is this: Is God the sovereign creator and sustainer of all things, or is man the measure of and sustainer of all things? Is man to humble himself and worship and serve the Creator, or is he to play the fool and worship and serve the creature?

In this lecture, Doug Phillips will introduce an ancient culture represented by ruins. He will explain how the Greek culture presents the antithesis to the biblical worldview and how men throughout history have attempted to revive and glorify some of the worst aspects of paganism. Mr. Phillips will also outline some of the major themes in the battle between Greco-Roman culture and Hebrew culture and show the dangers that come when men attempt to synchronize paganism with Christianity. The mouth that trumps the myth of glorious paganism will be stopped, as the glorious nature of the Hebrew thesis will be firmly established. In the end, the Christian will be challenged with this question: What do redeemed Christians have to do with the philosophies of pagan Greece, except to critique them and ultimately refute them?

LECTURE OUTLINE: JERUSALEM AND ATHENS

I. **Basic Presuppositions of Classical Greek Thinking vs. Hebrew Thinking?**
   A. Greek Thinking: "Man is the measure of all things"
      1. The Mind of Man: The highest value by which truth should be judged
      2. Man: The Ideal Standard
      3. Gods are a part of nature and under nature
      4. Neo-Platonic Idea: Dualism (mind is ideal; physical-bad; spiritual-good)
      5. Greek thought creates a tension between faith and reason
   B. A Christian view of history is framed by the works of God's providence
      1. God is the beginning and end of all things
      2. Man is a sinner dependent on God's redemption
      3. In Christian thought there is no tension between faith and reason

II. **Aquinas and His Syncretism of Christianity with Greek Philosophy**
   A. Aquinas borrowed directly from the philosophy of Aristotle
   B. Aquinas' view is the starting point of problematic apologetics
   C. God's purpose for the cosmos reveals an implicit duty to study, record, and redeem history (Eph 5:15; Psalm 39:4; Psalm 90:12)

III. **Themes in the Study of Greece**
   A. Historical overview of Greece and Greek thought
   B. Greek philosophy
   C. Primary philosophers
   D. Greek religion and mythology
   E. Greek evolution
   F. Greek art and culture
   G. The Gymnasium
   H. The Academy
   I. Hebrew syncretism with Greek philosophy
   J. Greek democracy
   K. Long-term influence of Greek thought on the West

IV. **Hebrew Syncretism**
   A. Last verses in the Old Testament
   B. Breakdown of families
   C. High point of Hellenistic influence on Jewish culture

V. **Hebraic Worldview vs. Greek Worldview**
   A. Hebrew-familistic vs. Greek-individualistic
   B. Hebrew worshiped One True God vs. Greek worshiped panoply of gods

C. Hebrew training (work and dominion) vs. Greek (philosophy and flesh)

VI. Religious Worldviews of Greeks

A. Statism: The state is the supreme authority over man

B. Civil Virtue: Individual piety defined in light of submission to the state

C. Humanism: Worship of man

VII. The Ideals of Classical Greek Paganism

A. Worship of body

B. Worship of the youth

C. Worship of the individual

D. Worship of the state

E. The superhero

F. Deification of athletics

G. Moral perversion

H. Philosophical dualism

VIII. Periods in Greek History

A. Early Greece: "The Trustee Period"

- 1200 BC: The Fall of Troy

- 900 BC: The rise of the (polis) Greek City-State

- 776 BC: The first Olympics

- 680 BC: Homer's *Odyssey*

- 620 BC: Drace's Laws of Athens

- 490 BC: The Battle of Marathon

- 480 BC: The Sea Battle of Salamis

- 461 BC: Athens vs. Sparta I, II

- 331 BC: Alexander conquers Persia

B. The Classical Period

- 500 BC: Beginning of Classical Period

- 399 BC: Death of Socrates

- 387 BC: Academy founded

- 347 BC: Death of Plato

- 333 BC: Jews under Greek rule

- 331 BC: Alexander conquers Persian Empire

- 323 BC: Alexander dies in Babylon (age 32)

- 322 BC: Aristotle dies

- 174 BC: Persecution of Jews by Antiochus that results in the Maccabean Revolt

IX. Jerusalem vs. Athens

A. Hebrew Republic vs. Greek Democracy

Much is said about the gift of "democracy" to the West from Ancient Greece. The evidence is clear that democracy was not favored by most, nor was it characteristic to the Greek society, where tyranny was more common than liberty. The rule of law, which characterized Medo-Persia, was in no sense a Hellenic way of life. Athens, supposedly the most enlightened, had a custom called ostracism, whereby any public man could be banished by vote ten years, later reduced to five. —Dr. R.J. Rushdoony

B.   Fatalism vs. Providence

Tragedy is not a biblical form of literature. Rather it is pagan, and sometimes in modern form it is very anti-Christian. Tragedy assumes that the universe is hostile to man. It does not see man as a sinner nor the universe as God-created and God-ruled. Instead, it sees man as a victim. The chorus in Sophocle's Oedipus the King declares, "Alas, ye generations of men, how mere a shadow do I count your life! Where, where is the mortal who wins more of happiness than just the seeming, and, after the semblance, a falling away? Thine is a fate that warns me, thine, thine unhappy Oedipus to call me earthly creature blest." The tragic view of life precedes the breakdown of culture because it encourages the belief that life is perverse and hopeless. —Dr. R.J. Rushdoony

X.   Icons of Greek Culture
A.   Plato
B.   The Gymnasium

XI.   Hebrew Syncretism

And to such a height did the passion for Greek fashions arise and the influx of foreign customs . . . that the priests were no longer interested in the services of the altar, but despising the sanctuary and neglecting the sacrifices, they hurried to take part in the unlawful displays held in the palaestra (wrestling arena) after the quoit throwing had been announced, thus setting at naught what their father honored and esteeming the glories of the Greeks about all else. —Second Book of Maccabees

QUESTIONS

1.   Who framed the question: "What indeed has Athens to do with Jerusalem?"

2.   How did Dr. Henry Van Til define culture?

3.   What is the highest standard by which truth should be judged according to the Greek worldview?

4.   What is Aquinas' theory of man, and what Greek formed his view?

5.   What is it meant by "Hebrew syncretism"?

6. What are three aspects of the Greek religious worldview?

7. Why did athletics play such an important role in Greek society?

8. Why is the Greek tragedy in direct opposition to biblical literature?

9. How does Greek democracy run contrary to the biblical concepts of liberty, order, and justice?

10. How does the Hebrew model for education differ from the Greek model for education?

GROUP DISCUSSION/ASSIGNMENT

1. In his book, *Liberty, Order, and Justice*, James McClellan notes that, while America's Founding Fathers were familiar with Greek literature and philosophy, James Monroe found the constitutions of ancient Greece to be "seriously flawed and not to be trusted by Americans." Moreover, Alexander Hamilton, John Jay, and James Madison each agreed that the ancient democracies of Greece were "turbulent" and were "unfit for the imitation, as they are repugnant to the to the genius of America." When John Adams critically examined twelve ancient democratic republics, he found them "all inferior to the political system of the new American republics in the several states. . . ." Later, Adams remarked "that he had learned from Plato two things only, that husbandmen and artisans should not be exempted from military service, and that hiccoughing may cure sneezing."[4] Discuss the attitude that the early American founders had toward Greek thought and democracy in contrast with the Hellenism of the Federal Period that soon followed after them.

2. In his work *Politics*, Aristotle wrote, "For as every household is a part of a State and the man and wife, father and children are parts of a household, and the excellence of any part must have reference to that of the whole, it is essential to educate our women and children with constant reference to the polity."[5] In the same work, he later wrote, "Again as the end proposed to the state as a whole is one, it is clear that the education of all the citizens must be one and the same and the superintendence of it a public affair rather than in private hands, as it now is, when each individual superintends his own children privately and with such private instruction he thinks good. . . . it is not right to suppose that any citizen is his own master, but rather that all belong to the State."[6] Contrast Aristotle's view of the family authority structure with the authority structure put forth for the family in 1 Corinthians 11:2-3. Also discuss Aristotle's view of education in light of the educational directives outlined in Deuteronomy 6:6-7.

3. The European Renaissance was characterized by a full embrace of everything Greco-Roman. Notably, this period is regarded by many today as a high watermark in human civilization. However, at the height of the Renaissance, an Augustinian monk wrote that Rome had been brought to openly exhibit the lowest forms of debauchery and pervasion. Rome became so decadent, he recorded, that it was commonly admitted in the streets, "If there be a hell, then Rome is built on top of it." This young man's name was Martin Luther. Discuss how the

Reformation stood in contrast to the Renaissance and how this contrast frames the epic battle between "Jerusalem and Athens."

4. The Greek mythology is perhaps best known by the interactions of "the gods" with the Greek supermen. The gods of the Greeks did not differ so greatly from men, and the super men of Greece did not differ so greatly from their gods. Significantly, the eminence of heroes such as Achilles and Hercules were attributed to the fact that they were *in part* divine. Perhaps the closest example in Scripture to a "superman" was Sampson, who drew supernatural strength from God. In contrast to the Greek superhero, Sampson was nothing of himself. Rather, his strength was completely dependent on the gift of grace from God. Yet both the Greek and Hebrew concept of the superhero was intrinsically religious. Our modern culture also has superheroes who derive their powers from the predominant religion of this age. DC Comics' Superman is the last member of a more highly-evolved race from another planet. Marvel's Spiderman is a young man who, when suffering a scientifically-engineered spider bite, underwent an evolutionary change. The X-Men are each representatives of the next step in man's evolution as they compete in a war of natural selection. Discuss how the concept of a superman is a deeply religious concept and identify what religion is reflected and promoted in modern superheroes. Furthermore, discuss the question: "What should Christians have to do with the modern demi-gods of secular humanist evolution?"

5. In Plato's *Republic*, the ruling class was to abstain from marriage, and the family was viewed as a hindrance to political duty. However, in Scripture we find that the Hebrew government was established as the heads of families and tribes were called upon to lead and take responsibility. Compare the view of the family in Plato's *Republic* with the view of the family represented in the Hebrew Republic. Which view was better represented in the founding of the American Republic? Discuss why the Roman Catholic practice of celibacy—along with the similar error taught in some Protestant circles—is preferred among the more "pious" and how this sentiment reflects a syncretism of Greek thought with Christian ministry.

SCRIPTURE READINGS

Romans 1

1 Corinthians 1

Acts 17

FURTHER READING

Tertullian: Pagan Philosophy, the Parent of Heresies

These are "the doctrines" of men and "of demons" produced for itching ears of the spirit of this world's wisdom: this the Lord called "foolishness," and "chose the foolish things of the world" to confound even philosophy itself. For (philosophy) it is which is the material of the world's wisdom, the rash interpreter of the nature and the dispensation of God. Indeed heresies are themselves instigated by philosophy. From this source came the Æons, and I know not what infinite forms, and the trinity of man in the system of Valentinus, who was of Plato's school. From the same source came Marcion's better god, with all his tranquility; he came of the Stoics. Then, again, the opinion that the soul dies is held by the Epicureans; while the denial of the restoration of the body is taken from the aggregate school of all the philosophers; also, when matter is made equal to God, then you have the teaching of Zeno; and when any doctrine is alleged touching a god of fire, then Heraclitus comes in. The same subject-matter is discussed over and over again by the heretics and the philosophers; the same are involved. Whence comes evil? Why is it permitted? What is the origin of man? and in what way does he come? Besides the question which Valentinus has very lately proposed—Whence comes God? Which he settles with the answer: From enthymesis and ectroma. Unhappy Aristotle! who invented for these men dialectics, the art of building up and pulling down; an art so evasive in its propositions, so far-fetched in its conjectures, so harsh, in its arguments, so productive of contentions—embarrassing even to itself, retracting everything, and really treating nothing! Whence spring those "fables and endless genealogies," and "unprofitable questions," and "words which spread like a cancer?" From all these, when the apostle would restrain us, he expressly names philosophy as that which he would have us be on our guard against. Writing to the Colossians, he says, "See that no one beguile you through philosophy and vain deceit, after the tradition of men, and contrary to the wisdom of the Holy Ghost." He had been at Athens, and had in his interviews (with its philosophers) become acquainted with that human wisdom which pretends to know the truth, whilst it only corrupts it, and is itself divided into its own manifold heresies, by the variety of its mutually repugnant sects. What indeed has Athens to do with Jerusalem? What concord is there between the Academy and the Church? what between heretics and Christians? Our instruction comes from "the porch of Solomon," who had himself taught that "the Lord should be sought in simplicity of heart." Away with all attempts to produce a mottled Christianity of Stoic, Platonic, and dialectic composition! We want no curious disputation after possessing Christ Jesus, no inquisition after enjoying the gospel! With our faith, we desire no further belief. For this is our palmary faith, that there is nothing which we ought to believe besides.

SCRIPTURE MEMORY

Colossians 2:8, "Beware lest any man spoil you through philosophy and vain deceit, after the tradition of men, after the rudiments of the world, and not after Christ."

Deuteronomy 4:5-7, "Behold, I have taught you statutes and judgments, even as the LORD my God commanded me, that ye should do so in the land whither ye go to possess it. Keep therefore and do them; for this is your wisdom and your understanding in the sight of the nations, which shall hear all these statutes, and say, Surely this great nation is a wise and understanding people. For what nation is there so great, who hath God so nigh unto them, as the LORD our God is in all things that we call upon him for?"

1 Chronicles 22:11-13, *"Now, my son, the LORD be with thee; and prosper thou, and build the house of the LORD thy God, as he hath said of thee. Only the LORD give thee wisdom and understanding, and give thee charge concerning Israel, that thou mayest keep the law of the LORD thy God. Then shalt thou prosper, if thou takest heed to fulfil the statutes and judgments which the LORD charged Moses with concerning Israel: be strong, and of good courage; dread not, nor be dismayed."*

DEFINITIONS

Civil Virtue: The idea that all righteousness and virtue in man is relative to his social and political environment.

Hellenization: A process by which a culture seeks to align itself with characteristics of pagan Greek culture.

Statism: The belief that the state has ultimate power and authority to direct every aspect of life.

Syncretism: The combination of dissimilar ideas or faith presuppositions.

SUMMARY

One of the most important lessons any student of history must learn is that culture is religion externalized. If a historian desires to evaluate a particular culture or civilization, he must do so by looking to the predominant religious presuppositions of that civilization. Man is supremely a religious and not merely a social creature. Consequently, he will develop an idea of what is ultimate in the universe. From this ultimate, he will develop a standard of ethics and laws consistent with the supremacy of that ultimate. Finally, man will attempt to apply that standard to every area of life and thought. The culture of a society of men, then, is developed and driven by the predominant religious presuppositions of that society.

In twenty-first-century America, a gradual Hellenization has taken place that has culminated in an abandonment of the family, liberty, and morality for humanism, statism, and decadence. It has become popular among historians today to praise and venerate the paganism of civilizations such as the Greeks, the Romans, the Celts, and the American Indians. Yet most if not all of these histories turn a blind eye to the human degradation which emanated from these cultures. Secular humanism reveres paganism because it shares its religious presuppositions. Yet ideas have inescapable consequences, and the civilization that embraces the paganism of the ancients will inevitably share in their legacies of tyranny, slavery, and perversion. There is no glory to be found in paganism and no grandeur to be found in a civilization without Christ.

BIBLIOGRAPHY

The Great Christian Revolution, by Otto Scott

Jerusalem and Athens, by Dr. Cornelius Van Til

The Calvinistic Concept of Culture, by Dr. Henry Van Til

Defeating the Myth-Storyians, By Joel McDermon

The Emergence of Liberty, by Douglas Kelly

END NOTES

1. Robert Stewart, ed., *Poems and Tales of Edgar Allen Poe* (Richmond, VA: B.F. Johnson Publishing Co., 1911), p .30.

2. Otto Scott, *The Great Christian Revolution* (Federal Way, WA: Uncommon Books, 1994) pp. 1-2.

3. Henry R. Van Till, *The Calvinist Concept of Culture,* (Grand Rapids, MI: Baker Book House, 1972), p. 200

4. James McClellan, *Liberty, Order, and Justice* (Indianapolis, IN: Liberty Fund, Inc., 2000), p.16.

5. Aristotle, *Politics*, Benjamin Jowett, trans. (Oxford: Clarendon Press, 1908), Book I, chapter xiii.

6. *Ibid.*, Book V, chapter i.

NOTES

CHAPTER 5

THE MYTH OF CULTURAL NEUTRALITY

INTRODUCTION

> *In this year Beorhtric [king of Wessex] took to wife Eadburh, daughter of King Offa. And in his days came first three ships of the Norwegians from Horthaland: and then the reeve rode thither and tried to compel them to go to the royal manner, for he did not know what they were: and they slew him. These were the first ships of the Danes to come to England.*
> —The Anglo-Saxon Chronicle *(AD 789)*

This excerpt from the *Anglo-Saxon Chronicle* is representative of the early tremors of a terrible earthquake that would shake all of Europe a generation later as the Viking rampage ensued. These "sea-borne pagans", as they would later be called, would make their ascension on the eve of Charlemagne's empire. The Vikings would test the resolve of kings from the gallantry of Alfred the Great to the cowardice of Charles the Fat, and they would become the subject of ardent missionary endeavors which would eventually lead to the conversion of a nation and the transformation of a national culture.

The Vikings were descendants of the Germanic line which inhabited Scandinavia and the Jutland peninsula. They were divided into three distinct groups: the Danes, the Norse, and the Swedes.

While these Scandinavians were able to avoid the pagan influences of Greece and Rome almost entirely, they maintained a paganism all of their own.[1] The ninth and tenth centuries are thoroughly replete with the violent despoil of the Northman. Their religion was war, and their culture was saturated with blood feuds, human sacrifice, slavery, and murder. Unlike other armies in Europe during that time, the Vikings did not spare women or children and had no scruples when it came to pillaging and burning the churches of God. Famines were an annual occurrence, and whole towns and provinces vanished away, owing to the ravishing of the Vikings across the European theater.

There are several theories that attempt to explain why the Vikings, who up to that time were primarily traders, suddenly thrust themselves into plunder. Arguably, one of the best explanations is based on the combination of political unrest, paganism, and exiles so common in Scandinavia during that period. Powerful men who were forced to flee into exile took fleets of armed men with them. At the time, their paganism translated into a cultural lust for war and plunder that they viewed as a necessity for survival.

One of the greatest providential developments that occurred during the Viking threat was a massive power-shift in the church and the state on the main continent of Europe. At the death of Charlemagne, the Holy Roman Empire was to be divided between his three sons. However, two of Charlemagne's sons had died, leaving the empire to his son Louis, later called "The Pious". Almost immediately, Louis moved to unite the empire into a single, indivisible, central power dominated by the Emperor. A similar transformation was to take place in the church, and power was to be dominated by Rome. However, this caused great unrest throughout the empire as the expansion was seen as an infringement on private property and individual liberty. This political unrest, combined with the attacks of the Vikings from without, led to the decentralization of the empire. The brief manifestation of centralized power was followed by a fragmentation of the empire into thousands of smaller units, as individuals united under local strongmen for protection of their private property and liberty. This was the dawn of the Feudal Age.

Yet perhaps the greatest insight that the Vikings can provide the historian is the affect that the Gospel of Christ has on national cultures. From very early on, the Europeans took a two-pronged approach to solving the Viking problem. First, they took care to build strong fortifications to repel the attacks, and men united with the local strongmen to train at arms to defend their families. This development led to the building of many thousands of strongholds throughout Europe and the rise of a class of citizen soldiers to defend them. Secondly, kings and missionaries alike made bold efforts to evangelize the Viking hordes and win them to Christ.

Christian evangelization made inroads with the Norsemen in three distinct ways. First, there were missionaries who brought the Gospel into the heathen lands, such as the bold Northumbrian Willibrord who preached the gospel of Christ to Ongendus, a Viking king described as "fiercer than a wild beast and harder than any stone."[2] Second, as the Vikings engaged in trade with the Christians, they brought back the testimony that these Christian traders bore out to them. Similarly, as the Vikings plundered European cities, they carried off women and children to be their slaves or wives. The faith of these captives was unshaken, and many of the Viking men were won to Christ through the steadfast witness of their wives or bondmen. Third, the Vikings began to settle in the lands that they had conquered, Britain in particular. When the Norsemen took root there, they were exposed to the strong Christian influence planted in the British Isles centuries before by men like Patrick and Columba. By the ninth century, "Christianity was firmly rooted in Scotland," noted one writer. "The speed with which the Scandinavian settlers were assimilated to it is testimony to this."[3]

Shortly before 1000 AD, the kings of Sweden, Norway, and Denmark accepted baptism. During one great sea battle in this year of wonders, Jarl Erik Haakonson replaced his "stem dweller," an image of Thor, with a cross. It was during these last years of the tenth century that the Vikings gave up on their old gods, Odin, Thor, and Freya.[4]

This abandonment of paganism for the lordship of Christ had a radical effect on the Scandinavian culture. While there were still remote traces of paganism among some of the Vikings, Christianity had become the predominant worldview. Consequently, the rape, pillage, and murder came to an end. Man-stealing and human sacrifices also ceased. The concept of private property which had been frowned on by many Viking groups was embraced and respected. Danish law, art, education, and economics changed with its embrace to Christianity. The Scandinavians would continue to play an important and influential in the course of European history and stand as a lasting testimony of the redeeming influence of the gospel on even the most barbaric of nations.

In this lecture, Col. John Eidsmoe will talk about the early culture of the Vikings. He will explain the deeply-rooted system of paganism which drove the Vikings to their ravaging of Europe. Col. Eidsmoe will also discuss how the Vikings were converted and how the redeemed Norsmen were used by God to shape the course of world history.

LECTURE OUTLINE: THE VIKINGS

I. **Introduction to the Vikings**
    A. The Vikings made several contributions
        1. Legal system
        2. Navigation
        3. Concept of human freedom
    B. Odin was a great warrior who became revered as a God
    C. The Norse were of the Germanic family

II. **Viking Rule of Law**
    A. Highly organized and very disciplined
    B. Centered very much on the liberty of the individual
    C. Government was decentralized

III. Mythology of the Vikings
    A. Polytheistic but believed in one supreme god and many lesser gods

    B. Gods were highly personal

    C. Religion was highly deterministic

    D. World was created by frost giants

    E. Vikings believed in three levels of existence

    F. The Vikings believed in two classes of gods

    G. Eschatology of the Vikings was pessimistic

IV. Freedom among the Vikings
    A. The southern European concept of liberty ended with Alexander the Great

    B. The concept of individual liberty is preserved among the Celts and Germans

V. Legal System of the Vikings
    A. Rulers governed by the consent of the governed

    B. Local town council maintained primary authority, even over the king

    C. There was a parliamentary system

    D. Law was oral and not written

    E. Crimes were tried by juries made up of statesmen and witnesses

VI. Core Values among the Vikings
    A. Courage

    B. Keeping one's word

    C. Hospitality

    D. Family

    E. Vengeance

VII. Evangelization of the Vikings
    A. King Olaf of Norway

    B. Iceland converted

    C. Greenland converted

VIII. Settlements of the Vikings
    A. Iceland

    B. Greenland

    C. Russia

    D. Scotland

    E. Normandy

IX. Manners and Customs among the Vikings
    A. Highly literate and wrote poetry

    B. Chess was a common game among the Norse

C.   Vikings were experts in siege warfare

D.   Vikings were very disciplined

QUESTIONS

1.   What are some of the major contributions of the Vikings?

2.   How was the paganism of the Greeks and the Viking similar?

3.   What was the parliamentary body of the Vikings called?

4.   What did the Vikings believe about the end of the world?

5.   How were the juries of the Vikings different from American juries?

6.   How did Alexander the Great betray the concept of individual liberty?

7.   Who was the first King of Norway to convert to Christianity?

8.   What drove the Vikings from North America?

9.   What are a few of the nations settled by the Vikings?

10. What major city did the Vikings take for the king of Jerusalem?

GROUP DISCUSSION/ASSIGNMENT

1.   King Alfred the Great was able to unite Britain and neutralize the Viking aggression against seemingly impossible odds. Alfred was a city planner and was one of the first in England to organize cities into grids. He built strongholds throughout the land to make it difficult for any invading army to plunder the inhabitants. Yet arguably the greatest contribution that Alfred made was to build up the church and increase literacy. Alfred translated the sacred books from Latin and made them accessible to commoners. Alfred also wrote books, and the *Anglo-Saxon Chronicle* is thought by some to have originated from his court. Discuss the importance of healthy churches and sound Christian scholarship to the nation. Contrast this with Marxism which is hostile to the church and is strengthened by illiteracy.

2.   Olaf, the first Christian king of Norway, took extensive measures to rid his lands of paganism. In one account, Olaf personally cut down an image of the Norse god Frey. Frey was the Norse god of the sun, rain, and fruitfulness. As Olaf approached the image he shouted, "'Now I will test Frey, if thou canst talk and answer me.' Frey was silent. 'If thou,' said the king, 'canst not or wilt not, then may the one who is in thee, and has long strengthened thee, answer me.' Frey was silent. The king said: 'Still I speak to thee, Frey; if thou canst give to men strength and power, then spare it not, and do what you are able to do, and if thou sleepest, awake and defend thee, for now I will attack thee.'"[5] King Olaf then took up his battleaxe and cut the idol into pieces in the sight of the people. This scene is not at all dissimilar to the kings of Israel who obeyed God

in ridding the land of idolatry by tearing down images and high places. Discuss this practice in contrast to the doctrine of religious pluralism so popular in modern culture.

3. During the close of the first millennium AD, Christian kings would practice a rite called *prima signatio*. When a pagan king was defeated on a field of battle and desired to surrender, the Christian king would call for his baptism as a sign of submission. *Prima signatio* did not indicate that the pagan king had become a Christian, rather it signified that the pagan king and all of his realm would submit to Christian dominion and the Christian rule of law. This was particularly instrumental to Alfred the Great who understood that all law is religious and was able to maintain the rule of law in lands where a multitude of Vikings had settled. Discuss this in light of the modern myth that non-Christians cannot be expected to obey Christian laws, and that morality cannot be legislated.

4. In his book *Christ and Culture*, H. Richard Niebuhr divides the Christian approach to culture into three categories. The first approach is "Christ against Culture". According to this view, Christ is separate and opposed to all culture. Those who espouse this view retreat from the culture and see culture as an evil creation of mankind. The second approach is the "Christ of Culture". According to this view, Christ is a creation of culture, and His identity is determined by the trends and norms of culture. Those who espouse this view consider the culture superior to Christ and as definitive as to the nature of Christ. The final approach is "Christ over Culture". According to this approach, Christ is the Lord over culture. He does not stand against it, nor is He subject to its influence; instead He is sovereign over it. Those who advocate this view seek to engage the culture and transform it in a manner that will bring glory to God. Which approach is consistent with the nature of Christ's rule as described in Psalm 110? Discuss which approach is illustrated by the evangelism and conversion of the Viking national culture.

SCRIPTURE READINGS

Matthew 28

Acts 1-2

FURTHER READING

John Calvin: Commentary on Matthew 28

Go out, therefore, and teach all nations. Though Mark, after having related that Christ *appeared to the eleven disciples,* immediately subjoins the command to *preach the gospel,* he does not speak of these as an unbroken series of events, for we learn from the enumeration of them which is given by Matthew, that the latter event did not take place before they had gone *into Galilee.* The meaning amounts to this, that by proclaiming the gospel everywhere, they should bring *all nations* to the obedience of the faith, and next, that they should seal and ratify their doctrine by the sign of the gospel. In Matthew, they are first taught simply to *teach*; but Mark expresses the kind of doctrine, that they should *preach the gospel*; and shortly afterwards Matthew himself adds this limitation, to *teach them to observe all things whatsoever the Lord hath commanded*.

Teaching them to observe all things. By these words, as I have formerly suggested, Christ shows that, in sending the apostles, he does not entirely resign his office, as if he ceased to be the Teacher of his Church; for he sends away the apostles with this reservation, that they shall not bring forward their own inventions, but shall purely and faithfully deliver from hand to hand (as we say) what he has entrusted to them. Would to God that the Pope would subject to this rule the power which he claims for himself; for we would easily permit him to be the successor of Peter or of Paul, provided that he did not usurp a tyrannical dominion over our souls. But as he has set aside the authority of Christ, and infects the Church with his childish fooleries, this shows plainly enough how widely he has departed from the apostolic office. In short, let us hold that by these words teachers are appointed over the Church, not to put forward whatever they may think proper, but that they, as well as others, may depend on the mouth of the Master alone, so as to gain disciples for him, and not for themselves.

And, lo, I am with you always. As Christ gave to the apostles a commission which they were unable to discharge by reliance on merely human power, he encourages them by the assurance of his heavenly protection. For before promising that he would be with them, he began with declaring that he is the, King *of heaven and earth*, who governs all things by his power and authority.

The pronoun *I* must be viewed as emphatic; as if he had said that the apostles, if they wished zealously to perform their duty, must not consider what they are able to do, but must rely on the invincible power of those under whose banner they fight. The nature of that presence which the Lord promises to his followers ought to be understood spiritually; for it is not necessary that he should descend from heaven in order to assist us, since he can assist us by the grace of his Spirit, as if he stretched out his hand from heaven. For he who, in respect of his body, is at a great distance from us, not only diffuses the efficacy of his Spirit through the whole world, but even actually dwells in us.

Even to the end of the world. It ought likewise to be remarked, that this was not spoken to the apostles alone; for the Lord promises his assistance not for a single age only, but *even to the end of the world*. It is as if he had said, that though the ministers of the gospel be weak and suffer the want of all things: he will be their guardian, so that they will rise victorious over all the opposition of the world. In like manner, experience clearly shows in the present day, that the operations of Christ are carried on wonderfully in a secret manner, so that the gospel surmounts innumerable obstacles.

SCRIPTURE MEMORY

Genesis 1:28, "And God blessed them, and God said unto them, Be fruitful, and multiply, and replenish the earth, and subdue it: and have dominion over the fish of the sea, and over the fowl of the air, and over every living thing that moveth upon the earth."

Genesis 9:1-3, "And God blessed Noah and his sons, and said unto them, Be fruitful, and multiply, and replenish the earth. And the fear of you and the dread of you shall be upon every beast of the earth, and upon every fowl of the air, upon all that moveth upon the earth, and upon all the fishes of the sea; into your hand are they delivered."

Proverbs 21:30, "There is no wisdom nor understanding nor counsel against the LORD."

DEFINITIONS

Cultural Mandate: The mandate given to Christians by Christ to preach the gospel to all nations, teaching them to observe those things He commanded which in turn creates a fundamental transformation in the culture.

Cultural Equality: The myth that equal rights of survival and respect should be given to all cultures, and that no one culture is to be viewed as superior over another.

SUMMARY

The testimony of the Viking conversion is an important one in light of the modern myth of cultural equality. In opposing the myth of cultural equality, it is important to underscore that the Christian does not oppose the concept of racial equality; indeed all men are created equal of one blood. Rather, the Christian view of history is quick to emphasize that there are definitive elements in Christian culture, the outworking of which will create a superior culture without regard to tribe, tongue, or nation. The Viking culture bears this out plainly.

Prior to its transformation, the Viking culture was deeply rooted in paganism. Private property was not protected; human life was of little value; violence and profanity was a cultural norm. However, due to the ardent and diligent missionary efforts of the Christians from surrounding nations, the Viking culture was transformed into a culture in which private property was protected, human life was sacred, and peace and order became the cultural anticipation.

The cultural mandate is not binding only on a few generations of Christians, but for all Christians to the end of the age. The Christian historian must look at cultural norms throughout history in light of the Gospel itself and understand the Kingdom of Christ as advancing throughout history for the transformation of cultures to reflect His glory.

BIBLIOGRAPHY

The Northmen, by Paul Christian Sinding

The Greatness of the Great Commission, by Kenneth L. Gentry

By This Standard, by Dr. Greg Bahnsen

The Rise of Paganism, by Jonathan Skinner

Evangelism and the Sovereignty of God, by J.I. Packer

END NOTES

1. Ross W. Collins, *A History of Medieval Civilization in Europe* (Boston, MA: Ginn and Company, 1936), p. 209.

2. Gwyn Jones, *A History of the Vikings* (New York, NY: Oxford University Press, 1973), p. 106.

3. Richard Fletcher, *The Barbarian Conversion* (New York, NY: Henry Holt and Co., 1997), p. 170.

4. Richard Erdoes, *AD 1000* (San Francisco, CA: Harper & Row Publishers, 1988), p. 137.

5. *Ibid.*, p. 143.

NOTES

NOTES

CHAPTER 6

IDEAS HAVE CONSEQUENCES

INTRODUCTION

In 1095, Pope Urban II made an arduous journey across the Alps and called for the Council of Clermont. It was there, on the plains just outside the city wall, that Urban II gave his famous call to arms. "An accursed race, a race wholly alienated from God violently invaded the lands of those Christians and has depopulated them by pillage and fire," explained Urban. "They have led away a part of the captives into their own country, and a part have they have killed by cruel tortures. They have either destroyed the churches of God or appropriated them for the rites of their own religion." Urban then urged the large group of clergy and knights to join the crusade:

> *Enter upon the road to the Holy Sepulcher; wrest that land from the wicked race. . . .*
> *Undertake this journey eagerly for the remission of your sins, and be assured of the reward of*
> *imperishable glory in the kingdom of Heaven. Dieu li volt—"God wills it".*[1]

The following summer, four armies totaling around 100,000 men-at-arms entered upon that road to the holy sepulcher, and the First Crusade had begun. The record of the Crusades has been dominated by a cynical view of history. Yet the Crusades were not created in a vacuum, and to attribute the launching of the Crusades to this single event alone is to tear the occurrence away from its broader historical context. First, one must recognize that the Crusades were in part fueled by intense religious persecution, mass genocide, and plundering that had raged throughout the Middle East and Africa in the name of Islam over a long period. The question of the Christian's duty to take up arms to defend and protect brothers and sisters in a far off land had been a point of almost constant debate for years. Secondly, the continual threat of Islamic invasion from the east of Europe and from Sicily had sparked several smaller-scale holy wars prior to the First Crusade. Legal scholar Harold Berman points out that:

> Forty years before the papacy summoned the whole of Western Christendom to a crusade for the liberation of Palestine, Robert Guiscard and Roger [de Hauteville] viewed their campaigns as Holy Wars. Embarking on battles against Moslem forces, they exhorted their followers to fight as soldiers of the army of Christ. In describing Robert Guiscard's preparations to invade Sicily, his chronicler quotes him as saying, "My desire is to deliver Catholics and Christians from the Saracens and to be an instrument of God's vengeance."[2]

Thirdly, the Great Schism between the East and West church had taken place just forty-one years earlier in 1054. It is said that one of Urban's key motives for launching a crusade was to aid the Byzantine Empire in driving out the Moslem Turks from Asia Minor. Through this act of deliverance it was hoped that the Greek Church would finally recognize the supremacy of the Church in Rome.[3] Finally, the amount of violent conflict which took place inside Europe was substantial. The Crusades provided an opportunity for all of Europe to leave off fighting each other and to unite together against a common enemy.

While there are many criticisms to be made about the motives and nature of the Crusades, it is important to note that some of the most common charges lodged by modern historians are mischaracterizations at best. For instance, the original motives for launching the Crusades had very little, if anything, to do with converting unbelievers at the edge of the sword. This characterization more aptly represents the Muslims of that period who had never converted any nation except by conquest. In fact, an honest treatment will indicate that the motives for launching the First Crusade were not so different from the motives nations engage themselves in modern wars.

The most glaring criticisms that can be made of the Crusades are the various inconsistencies with biblical theology and Christian character. Martin Luther, among other Protestant Reformers, drew attention to these problems. On June 15, 1520, Pope Leo X delivered the *Exsurge Domine*, calling Luther to recant his teaching under threat of excommunication, in part because he had criticized the Crusades and the theological fallout that had sprung from them. Luther had taught that heaven is not guaranteed by any works of man; that "the Roman Pontiff . . . is not the vicar of Christ over all the churches of the entire world"; and that "the treasures of the Church, from which the pope grants indulgences, are not the merits of Christ . . . of no avail to those who truly gain them."[4] When asked to recant, Luther publicly burned his copy of the *Exsurge Domine* and did the same with the *Decet Romanun Pontificem* issued to excommunicate him just six months later. It is important to take notice that these deep-rooted errors confronted by Luther during the Reformation are the same errors we discover as mere saplings at Clermont just over four hundred years earlier.

"Undertake this journey eagerly for the remission of your sins," urged Urban II that day at Clermont, "and be assured of the reward of imperishable glory in the kingdom of Heaven." The proposition that the remission of sin could be achieved by the good work of making a crusade to the Holy Land helped lay the foundation of errors which would be ardently opposed by the Reformation. At Clermont, Urban II laid the antithesis to the doctrine that salvation was by grace through faith in Jesus Christ alone, for the glory of God alone, according to the testimony of Scripture alone. In addition, the Pope, who was in effect now commanding all the armies of Western Europe, signaled a new chapter in the road to papal supremacy and laid the groundwork for the future sale of indulgences. One biographer of Luther states:

> *This was the seed of the indulgence which would never have grown to its later enormous proportions had it not been for the crusades. Mohammed promised his followers paradise if they fell in battle against unbelievers, but Christian warriors were at first without this comforting assurance. Their faith was not long left in doubt, however, for as early as 855 Leo IV promised heaven to the Franks who died fighting Moslems. A quarter of a century later John VIII proclaimed absolution for all sins and remission of all penalties to soldiers of the holy war, and from that time on the "crusade indulgence" became a regular means of recruiting, used for example . . . by Urban II in 1095. . . . The means which had proved successful in getting soldiers for the crusade were first used in 1145 or 1146 to get money for the same end.[5]*

As the Crusades progressed from the First to the Ninth Crusade, including the smaller unnumbered engagements, the fruit of these errors becomes increasingly evident as accounts of abuse, corruption, and tyranny seemed to grow more prevalent with each successive "Holy War".

Modern cynics magnify these abuses to drown out the whole period from its historical context. If we are to truly understand the Crusades and the important lessons that they can teach us today, we must reject the cynical approach to historical interpretation.

In this lecture, Dr. George Grant will explain the political and religious tensions that brought the Crusades about. Dr. Grant will faithfully depict the actors at each end of the battlefield and discuss some of the errors that most modern historians make when studying the Crusades. Most importantly, Dr. Grant will demonstrate how understanding the Crusades is crucial to our understanding of culture today.

LECTURE OUTLINE: THE CRUSADES

I. **Islam: Salvation through Works**
    A. Five Pillars of Islam
        1. Shahada: Profession of faith
        2. Salat: Prayers
        3. Zakat: Giving of alms
        4. Sawm during Ramadan
        5. Hajj: Pilgrimage to Mecca

II. **Islam's Vision for "Jihad" (Holy War)**
    A. Jihad was to be pursued at all costs
    B. Martyrs were guaranteed paradise
    C. A military movement of which Christendom was the target

III. **Mohammed's Successor, Umar**
    A. Despised Christianity and sought to eradicate it from the world
    B. Conquered Syria, Egypt, and Byzantium (604–636)
    C. Persecuted, tortured, and enslaved the people he subjugated
    D. Paved the way for conquests in Europe

IV. **The Crusades in Context**
    A. Middle East was at one time Christian
    B. Islam subjugated the Christians by plunder and murder
    C. Conquest by Islam characterized by forced conversions

V. **The Crusades**
    A. The Council of Clermont (1095)
    B. First Crusade
        1. Established five Crusader kingdoms
        2. Recovered Jerusalem and Bethlehem (1099)
        3. Restoration of the land
    C. Second Crusade
        1. The Purpose: To recover Edessa
        2. Accomplished purpose in (1148)
    D. Third Crusade (1187)
        1. Involved Richard the Lionheart, Phillip II, and Fredrick the Great
        2. Jerusalem is lost
    E. Fourth Crusade (1198-1204)
        1. Internal war breaks out
        2. Marks the beginning of the end of the Medieval Period

F.   Fifth Crusade (1217)

G.   Sixth Crusade (1228)

H.   Seventh Crusade (1248)

I.   Eighth Crusade (1267)

VI.   **Conclusions**

A.   The Crusades were intended to recover Christianity in the Middle East

B.   Islam never converted nations; all Islam nations were conquered

C.   Islam has never produced a society of widespread freedom and prosperity

D.   John Calvin declared: "Until the Church finds the heart and the will to care for those lost souls bound in Islam with the hope of the Gospel, we shall always be at peril."

QUESTIONS

1.   How does Islam teach a doctrine of salvation by works?

2.   What are the characteristics of Jihad?

3.   How did Islam convert surrounding nations?

4.   What was the predominant religion in the Middle East prior to the Islamic conquest?

5.   What took place at the Council of Clermont in 1095?

6.   What kingdoms were established during the First Crusade?

7.   When was the Second Crusade launched?

8.   What chief city was lost during the Third Crusade?

9.   What was the intention of the Crusades?

10.   What was the opinion of the Reformers on the Crusades?

GROUP DISCUSSION/ASSIGNMENT

1.   For centuries, Europe has been threatened with Islamic invasion; however, in the last century, Europe abandoned the biblical family model and replaced it with the egalitarian model that considers marriage a contract for cohabitation. Consequently, fathers and mothers have left the home with no one to look after children. Europeans see children as a hindrance and are having fewer offspring as a result. Their Muslim population, on the other hand, has maintained a strong family that supports having many children. Significantly, it is projected that Europe will be predominantly Muslim by the year 2050. Discuss this trend of Muslim invasion in light of its historical context.

2.   At the Council of Trent, the Catholic Church condemned the Reformation, warning that "no one ought to flatter himself up with faith alone, fancying that by faith alone he is made an

heir. . . . If any one saith, that by the said sacraments of the New Law grace is not conferred through the act performed, but that faith alone in the divine promise suffices for the obtaining of grace; let him be anathema."[6] Discuss how this idea parallels the statement made by Pope Urban at Clermont: "Undertake this journey eagerly for the remission of your sins, and be assured of the reward of imperishable glory in the kingdom of Heaven."

3. Many historians characterize the Crusades as being an example of Christian aggression against Islamic nations who desired to live quietly and peaceably. This is false. As noted in this chapter, there are several factors that played a role in the determination of Europe to go to war, many of which are used as justifications by modern nations. Discuss whether or not these were justifiable reasons for war in light of Scripture.

4. Almost four hundred years after the beginning of the First Crusade, Columbus would sail to the New World. In 1574, Pope Gregory XIII would issue a Bull of Crusade for those sent to subjugate the New World for Spain. In contrast, England, greatly influenced by the Reformation, would send families instead of their armies. Discuss this model in light of the dominion mandate in Genesis 1:28.

5. Secular humanists often point out the inconsistencies which occurred during the Crusades as a means to criticize Christianity. However, evolutionists like Adolf Hitler, Joseph Stalin (along with the secular humanist practice of abortion) have made the last century the bloodiest century the world has ever known—far more violent, indeed, than four centuries of crusades. Discuss the hypocrisy of these secular humanist criticisms in light of this historical fact. Also discuss how this illustrates that ideas have consequences.

SCRIPTURE READINGS

Psalm 1

Psalm 145

FURTHER READING

Samuel Rutherford: Excerpt from the Trial & Triumph of Faith

This justification without faith, casteth loose the covenant, "I will be your God." But here a condition—God is not bound and we free; therefore this is the other part, "and ye shall be my people." Now, it is taught by libertines, that there can be no closing with Christ, in a promise that hath a qualification or condition expressed; and that conditional promises are legal. It is true, if the word "condition" be taken in a wrong sense, the promises are not conditional. For, 1st, Arminians take a condition for a free act, which we absolutely may perform or not perform by free will, not acted by the predeterminating grace of Christ; so jurists take the word: but this maketh men lords of heaven and hell, and putteth the keys of life and death over to absolute contingency. 2nd. Conditions have a Popish sense, for doing that which, by some merit, moveth God to give to men wages for work, and so, promises are not conditional: but libertines deny all conditions. But taking condition, for any qualification wrought in us by the power of the saving grace of God; Christ promiseth soul-ease, but upon a condition, which, I grant, his grace worketh, that the soul be sin-sick for Christ; and he offereth "wine and milk," (Isa. 55:1) "And the water of life freely," (Rev. 22:17) upon condition that you buy without money: no purse is Christ's grace-market, no hire and sense of wretchedness is a hire for Christ. And the truth is, it is an improper condition, if a father promise lands to a son, so he will pay him a thousand crowns for the lands; and if the Father of free grace can only, and doth give him the thousand crowns also: the payment is most improperly a hire or a condition, and we may well say, the whole bargain is pure grace; for both wages and work is free grace. But the ground of libertines is fleshly laziness, and to sin, because grace aboundeth; for they print it, that all the activity of a believer is to sin. So, to believe must be sin; to run the ways of God's commandments with a heart enlarged by grace, must be no action of grace, but an action of the flesh.

SCRIPTURE MEMORY

Romans 12:1-2, "I beseech you therefore, brethren, by the mercies of God, that ye present your bodies a living sacrifice, holy, acceptable unto God, which is your reasonable service. And be not conformed to this world: but be ye transformed by the renewing of your mind, that ye may prove what is that good, and acceptable, and perfect, will of God."

Ephesians 5:15-17, "See then that ye walk circumspectly, not as fools, but as wise, redeeming the time, because the days are evil. Wherefore be ye not unwise, but understanding what the will of the Lord is."

1 Peter 3:15, "But sanctify the Lord God in your hearts: and be ready always to give an answer to every man that asketh you a reason of the hope that is in you with meekness and fear."

DEFINITIONS

Cynical View of History: A negative or pessimistic view of history in which the historian fails to find perfection and turns to scornful skepticism with regard to history in general or particular peoples or periods of history.

Jihad: A holy war waged on behalf of Islam as a religious duty and spiritual discipline.

Just War Theory: An ethical doctrine which holds that wars and other military conflict for war are only morally justifiable when they meet the biblical allowances for armed resistance.

SUMMARY

Ideas have consequences, and the history of mankind cannot be separated from its theology. The major errors of the Crusades are not political in nature but rather theological in nature.

At Clermont, Urban II commissioned the nations in a Holy War which had its footing on an erroneous theological framework. Rome would be made to answer for this heretical teaching at the time of the Reformation.

The Crusades offer a number of valuable lessons for the observer. Key among them is this: that history does not take place in a vacuum; through God's Providence, it is the product of the theology and prevailing ideas of the time. In order for an historian of the Crusades, or any other period, to have a clear understanding of the history he is studying, he must become familiar with the theology and dominant ideas of the age under consideration. Regrettably, many historians today erroneously examine history in light of the prevailing ideas of our Modern Age, reading the present into the past. Not only does such a practice greatly impair the observer's ability to understand why an event took place, but it will also bar any understanding of the true significance of past events as they pertain to modern culture. Bad ideas have consequences, and those who fail to understand history in light of the prevailing ideas that characterized it are destined to adopt the same bad ideas and inherit the same bad consequences. By contrast, good ideas have good consequences, and those who learn from the godly examples of the past are destined to inherit the blessings of God.

BIBLIOGRAPHY

Ideas Have Consequences, by Richard Weaver

John Calvin and the Legacy of American Colonization, by Dan Ford

Law and Revolution, by Harold J. Berman

A Christian View of War, by Greg Bahnsen

The Christian Attitude toward War, by Loraine Boettner

END NOTES

1. William Safire, *Lend Me Your Ears: Great Speeches in History* (New York: W.W. Norton and Co., 2004), p. 94.

2. Harold J. Berman, *Law and Revolution* (Cambridge, MA: Harvard University Press, 1983), p. 410.

3. Andrew McCall, *The Medieval Underworld* (London: Hamish Hamilton Ltd., 1979), p. 89.

4. Hans J. Hillerbrand, *The Reformation in Its Own Words* (London: SCM Press, 1964), pp. 80-84.

5. Preserved Smith, *The Life and Letters of Martin Luther* (New York: Houghton Mifflin Co., 1914), p. 36.

6. *The Council of Trent*, Chapter XI Cannon IV, Theodore Alois Buckley, trans. (London: George Routledge and Co., 1851), pp. 81-82.

NOTES

NOTES

CHAPTER 7

HISTORY of DIVINE GRACE

INTRODUCTION

Scattered throughout central America are the decaying remnants of an ancient mystery civilization—a civilization which groaned out its last breath more than half a millennium ago and which now has been reclaimed by the landscape. The Mayan civilization was perhaps one of the most advanced civilizations of the ancient world. The traces of Mayan architecture, art, mathematics, astronomy, and every natural industry of an active society can be found buried in the silence of its own desolation. Perhaps the mood is captured best by explorer John Lloyd Stevens who said this at the time of his discovery of the Mayan city of Copan:

> *The city was buried in forest, and entirely hidden from sight. Imagination peopled the quarry with workman, and laid bare the city to their view. Here as the sculpture worked, he turned to the theater of his glory, as the Greek did to the acropolis of Athens, and dreamed of immortal fame. Little did he imagine that the time would come when his works would perish, his race be extinct, his city a desolation and abode for reptiles,—for strangers to gaze at, and wonder by what race it had once been inhabited.[1]*

Where are the Mayas? Where are the Babylonians, the Assyrians, the Greeks, and the Romans? Their confident boasts of security and invulnerability that once echoed through the great halls of civilization have fallen silent among the great ruins of the wilderness. Their empires have crumbled, and the inhabitants have been driven to the brink of extinction. Their gates have either been inhabited by their enemies or have been abandoned altogether to the wilds. Instead of an evolving culture, with the Mayas we find a culture highly advanced in science and technology, well educated, quickly devolving, and finally burning out. Today, those people who claim to be descendants of the Mayas, hold as a crowning honor their connection to a civilization that died out more than five hundred years ago. Yet the intricate stone palaces have now been abandoned for grass huts, and that civilization which was one of the most advanced in the ancient world is now one of the world's most crude.

The stony ruins of what was once the Mayan civilization is preserved as a testimony that all those who hate God love death[2], and a nation that rejects God's sovereignty over every area of life will descend into national and cultural decay. Hence, the Mayas present a dreadful warning for modern civilizations. Modern trends of statism, public education, athletic fanaticism, evolution, occultism, and child sacrifice each mirror patterns of Mayan self destruction. Modernity's boast that culture has evolved, and man has arrived at a place where faith in God is irrelevant in matters of life, law, and culture only serves to reverberate the blunder of the Mayan civilization. The longevity of nations is not based on military might, economic stability, or scientific and technological innovation, but rather on the grace and favor of God as they obey His law.

What we must recognize is this: Man, whether he names the name of Christ or not, is totally dependent on the grace of God. By one man's sin, sin passed upon all men, so that all mankind is utterly dead in trespass and sin. Therefore, an explanation must be given for the existence of virtue and progress among men, not only for man's progress, but also for man's ability even to comprehend progress at all. The presence of virtue and progress among a human race that is utterly incapable of it can only be explained in light of God's dispensation of grace. While the demonstration of that depravity rarely stoops to the level of dissipation evidenced by the Mayas, this fallen civilization stands as a testimony of the inclinations of the natural man apart from the restraint of God's common grace.

Apart from the demonstration of common grace, it is impossible to account for the existence of universal concepts such as civil order, marriage, personal property, economics, philosophy, ethics, reason, or any other establishment of moral order. Every aspect of reality is a product of the gracious providence of God and "in every distinguished act there is a special inspiration."[3] So, then, a rejection of the doctrines of grace made in the effort to elevate humanity is not only futile, but it rather marks man's descent into the most debased forms of savagery. In *To Be as God*, Dr. R.J. Rushdoony wrote:

> *The whole modern age, perhaps more so than previous ones because it has been so generously*
> *blessed by God's favors, is militantly anti-grace. The perspective of autonomy separates*
> *all spheres and all men and things from God, whereas the clear vision of grace is our total*

dependence on grace. But a world stripped of all grace would be no more than hell, and modern man's vision of life and the future is a hunger for hell. The Christian must separate himself from this disastrous goal. The dream of the Golden Age without God is a vision of hell.[4]

There are pervasive trends of this pursuit of human debasement and savagery throughout the labors of social Darwinism. Consider Margaret Mead's *Coming of Age in Samoa*, for example, a culture study of young girls raised in the crude culture on the islands of Samoa in the 1920s. Mead, who vehemently hated the grace of God as demonstrated in premarital chastity and Christian monogamy, sought to demonstrate that secular humanist cultures were superior to Christian cultures. For Mead, that meant traveling to the far reaches of the earth to seek out, study, and imitate rudimentary and savage cultures. (Note: In her pursuit to portray the "noble savage", Mead's research was significantly fabricated to reach her intended conclusion.) For Mead and her fellow evolutionists, the purest expression of man is to be found where there is little or no trace of God's common grace in a culture. Thus, modern man, through evolution, is thrown into a rapid descent into a new age of savagery and animalistic behavior.

In this lecture, Doug Phillips will tell the story of his journey to the ruins of the Ancient Mayas. He will explain the Mayan culture from the Cult of Kukulcan to their ultimate demise as they drank from waters polluted with the remains of their children. Finally, Mr. Phillips will show the vital importance of understanding what the Mayas mean for modern civilization, along with the role that every Christian must play in seeking to redeem civilization for Christ.

LECTURE OUTLINE: A TERRIFYING BEAUTY

I.   Introduction
   A.   Mayas were technologically advanced
   B.   Masters of aesthetics
   C.   Their savagery was such as the world has rarely seen
   D.   Their demise provides a great lesson for America

II.   To Be Discovered
   A.   There is much left to be discovered about the Mayan civilization
   B.   It was a civilization of pyramids and hieroglyphic writings
   C.   The Mayan civilization was very advanced mathematically
   D.   Journeys of John Lloyd Stephens
   E.   A call for Christian exploration

III. The Ruins of the Mayan Civilization
   A.   The landscape is covered with pyramids called ziggurats
   B.   There were observatories which resemble those of other mystery religions

C. The structure took generations to build

D. Images of snakes and skulls cover the structures

E. Mayas covered a large geographical location

IV. Where Did the Mayas Come From?

A. Most chronology based on false evolutionary presuppositions

B. Unlikely theory of an Ice Age land bridge

C. Theory that ancient man built ships to navigate the globe

D. Mayas had a unique language that originated at Babel

V. Connections with Babel

A. Global similarities exist all over the world

B. Temple and pyramid structures

C. Similarities in religious practices

    1. Astrology at the center

    2. Pyramids built for worship

    3. Records of Creation, Serpent, Fall, and the Flood

    4. Blood sacrifice and the worship of animals

VI. Chronology of the Mayas

A. It is not certain when the Mayan people arrived in Central America

B. Classical period (292 AD-593 AD)

C. Late Classical period (593 AD-899 AD)

D. Toltec influence (976 AD-1200 AD)

E. Spanish period (1500s)

F. Period of discovery (1800s)

VII. Mayan Technology

A. Written language

B. Buildings situated and constructed as astronomical observatories

C. Calendar system within .002 exactness of the modern calendar

D. The Mayas had a concept of the number 0

E. Time was very important to the Mayas

    1. Two calendars

    2. 365 days

VIII. Mayan and Meso-American Religious Connections with the Biblical Record of the Earth

A. Creation by a trinitarian serpent

B. Man created first, then woman

C. Flood legend

D. Confusion of the languages

IX. **The Cult of Kukulcan (Quetzalcoatl)**
  A. A snake deity to which the Mayas sacrificed their children
  B. Images are found throughout the Mayan structures
  C. Mayas believed the world has been created five times
  D. Most gods are reptilian
  E. Heaven only reserved for a few
  F. Human sacrifice by removing heart while the victim was still alive

X. **Structural Features of a Mayan City**
  A. The pyramid was a place of human sacrifice
  B. Buildings were situated to mirror astronomical predictions
  C. Buildings were also situated to manipulate and project acoustics
  D. Sports complexes were an important aspect of Mayan culture
  E. The skull motif represents warriors who have died

XI. **A World without Fathers and Sons**
  A. Children did not belong to the parents, but the priests
  B. The priests would select children to be sacrificed
  C. Many children were thrown into the water source which caused disease
  D. 80,000 people were sacrificed in four days by the Aztecs

XII. **Startling Conclusions**
  A. Cultures do not evolve
  B. Mayan Empire destroyed internally as an act of divine judgment

XIII. **Seven Messages of the Mayas**
  A. Culturally advanced and technologically and scientifically brilliant cultures are capable of remarkable atrocities
  B. Even cultures founded on godliness are capable of degenerating to such an extent that they promote as virtuous unspeakable horrors
  C. Ordinary men and women are capable of being so desensitized to evil that they tolerate, accept, and promote unthinkable atrocities
  D. One of the greatest dangers facing any society results when parents entrust their children to the state to be managed and educated by scientists/priests of a false religion
  E. Nations that worship athletics, ungodly violence, and communicate a fascination with death and darkness are well on their way to ritual public sacrifice and bloodsport
  F. God destroys and wipes from the earth those nations which engage in child sacrifice, idolatry, and perversion
  G. God chooses unusual and ironic instruments of judgment to chastise and punish those who despise Him and His law

XIV. Concluding Thoughts about American Culture
    A. America must humble itself and ask God for mercy

    B. We must exchange a culture of death for a culture of life

    C. America must repent and turn back to the law of God

QUESTIONS

1. What were some of the major advancements made by the Mayan civilization?

2. Why is it important for Christians to engage in archeology and exploration?

3. What structure is found all over the world as a result of the Babylonian Mystery Religion?

4. What are some of the ways that the Mayan people could have migrated to South America?

5. What are two of the most predominant symbols used in Mayan art and architecture?

6. What was one of the affects of the breakdown of the Mayan families?

7. What Mayan legends are similar to the record of Scripture?

8. What does the Mayan culture teach us about the myth of cultural evolution?

9. What is believed to be the cause of the sudden demise of the Mayan culture?

10. Why is God's Law important to every nation?

GROUP DISCUSSION/ASSIGNMENT

1. The building of Noah's Ark required an extraordinary amount of skill and knowledge on the part of Noah and his sons. This knowledge would have survived the Flood and been passed on to future generations. Discuss this fact in light of the technology demonstrated in ancient cultures, technology which often baffles modern social evolutionists. Also discuss how this might have played a part in transplanting the Mayan people to a new continent.

2. Child sacrifice was practiced in cultures all around the world from the Babylonians in the Middle East to the Mayas on the American Continent. In our modern culture, we often assume that child sacrifice is something that we in the West have outgrown. Discuss how the widespread practice of abortions conflicts with this assumption.

3. In the Mayan culture, the high priest was also the teacher in their system of state education. This parallels our own time in that early American state educators can be found calling teachers and scientists the "high priests" of modernity. Discuss the similarity of this modern boast with what we know of the priests/educators of the Mayas.

4. One of the most haunting aspects about the Mayan culture was the manner in which they had become desensitized to public murder, mutilation, and cannibalism. It is baffling to many modern minds how they could embrace such grotesque practices as a way of life. Yet while

we are far removed in modern culture from pagan altars and coliseums where bloodsport is heralded, the depiction of such violence, gore, and horror is often depicted and celebrated in the modern cinema. Discuss how we have become desensitized to gore and nudity through modern forms of entertainment.

SCRIPTURE READINGS

Leviticus 18:20-28

2 Chronicles 7:13-20

Isaiah 24:1-6

FURTHER READING

Rev. George Gillespie: Truth and Heresy

We run a great hazard of our souls and our salvation when we turn aside from truth to error. It is said of the unstable, that they wrest the scriptures "unto their own destruction," 2 Pet. 3:16. Like a man fallen into quicksands, the more he wrestles out the more he sinks. When the apostle has spoken of Christ's purchasing of our reconciliation, justification and sanctification, he adds an if; Col. 1:23, "If ye continue in the faith grounded and settled, and be not moved away from the hope of the gospel, which ye have heard." Not that our persevering in the true faith was a condition in Christ's purchasing of these blessings, but it is a condition without which we cannot possess and enjoy what Christ has purchased; that is, he that falls away from the true doctrine of the gospel proves himself to have no part of the benefits of Christ.

Some errors are, in their own nature, damnable and inconsistent with the state of grace or fellowship with God, 2 Peter 2:9; so 2 John 9, "Whosoever transgresseth and abideth not in the doctrine of Christ, hath not God." Sure it may be said of Arians, Socinians, Papists, Libertines, they have not God, because they abide not in the doctrine of Christ; so Gal. 5:4. Other errors there are, of which I may say, whatsoever they are comparatively, impenitency, and continuing in them, does condemn, whence it is that the apostle James reckons him who errs from the truth to be in a way of death and danger of damnation, James 5:19-20.

Now, the preservatives against wavering, and helps to steadfastness in the faith, are these: 1. Grow in knowledge and circumspection; be not simple as children in understanding. There is "sleight of men, and cunning craftiness, whereby they lie in wait to deceive;" so speaks the apostle of those that spread diverse and strange doctrines, Eph. 4:14; and Rom. 16:18, he warns us that they do "by good words and fair speeches deceive the hearts of the simple." You have, therefore, need of the wisdom of the serpent, that you be not deceived, as well as of the simplicity of the dove, that you be not a deceiver, Phil. 1:9-10.

Do not rashly engage into any new opinion, much less into the spreading of it. With the well-advised is wisdom. Pythagoras would have his scholars only to hear, and not to speak for five years. Be swift to hear, but not to speak or engage: "Prove all things," and when you have proved, be sure to "hold fast to that which is good," 1 Thess. 5:21; Matt. 7:15, 17. There was never a heresy yet broached, but under some fair plausible pretence: "beguiling unstable souls," as Peter speaks, 2 Peter 2:14. "The simple believeth every word," Prov. 14:15. Be not like the two hundred that went in the "simplicity" of their hearts after Absalom in his rebellion, not knowing anything, but that he was to pay his vow in Hebron, 2 Sam. 15:11.

SCRIPTURE MEMORY

Luke 1:50-52, "And his mercy is on them that fear him from generation to generation. He hath shewed strength with his arm; he hath scattered the proud in the imagination of their hearts. He hath put down the mighty from their seats, and exalted them of low degree."

Malachi 4:1, "For, behold, the day cometh, that shall burn as an oven; and all the proud, yea, and all that do wickedly, shall be stubble: and the day that cometh shall burn them up, saith the LORD of hosts, that it shall leave them neither root nor branch."

James 4:5-7, "Do ye think that the scripture saith in vain, The spirit that dwelleth in us lusteth to envy? But he giveth more grace. Wherefore he saith, God resisteth the proud, but giveth grace unto the humble. Submit yourselves therefore to God. Resist the devil, and he will flee from you."

DEFINITIONS

Common Grace: The measure of grace issuing from "the light of nature, and the works of creation and providence, do so far manifest the goodness, wisdom, and power of God, as to leave men inexcusable; yet are they not sufficient to give that knowledge of God, and of his will, which is necessary unto salvation" (Westminster Confession of Faith 1:1).

Noble Savage Theory: The mythical notion that the purest ideal of man is expressed by a humanity that is unencumbered by the influence of civilization.

Cultural Relativism: The misconception that the actions of a civilization are to be judged in terms of its own ethical standards; that outside standards of ethics (such as God's law) should not be imposed to determine the morality of a culture.

SUMMARY

When the Spanish first encountered Mayan culture, the Mayas were strangely on the brink of extinction. Today the ruins of that broken civilization stand as a perpetual witness of the inevitable fate of a people who become opposed to all works of grace. The grace of God is essential to the health and longevity of any civilization. Without the restraining grace of God, a culture will fall deeper and deeper into its own total depravity.

For the historian, civilizations cannot be rightly understood until they are held up to the light of God's Word. A civilization like that of the Mayas may boast impressive technology, art, architecture, and political strength. Yet no civilization can attain any of these things apart from the grace of God. Therefore, once God's law is rejected, and grace is removed from a culture, all of the education, art, technology and political strength of that culture will not be able to sustain it.

A culture without grace will descend into total savagery and decadence. The Mayan testimony stands today as a stern warning to modern nations who have the audacity to look to their technology, economies, science, education systems and political power and boast. Inasmuch as modern civilizations demonstrate an ongoing and entrenched hostility to the work of grace, they are destined to share a future with the Mayas—alone, isolated, and unpopulated in the silence of obscurity.

BIBLIOGRAPHY

Incidents of Travel in Central America, Chiapas, and Yucatan, by John Lloyd Stevens

Maps of the Ancient Sea Kings, by Charles H. Hapgood

Always Ready, by Dr. Greg Bahnsen

Christianity: A Total World and Life System, by Abraham Kuyper

After the Flood, by Bill Cooper

END NOTES

1. John Lloyd Stevens, *Incidents of Travel in Central America Chiapas, and Yucatan* (London: Arthur Hall, Virtue & Co., 1854), pp. 89-90.

2. Prov. 8:36

3. John Calvin, *Institutes of the Christian Religion*, Henry Beveridge, trans. (Grand Rapids, MI: Wm. B. Eerdmans Publishing Company, 1953), Bk. II, Ch. 2, Sec. 17.

4. R.J. Rushdoony, *To Be as Gods* (Vallecito, CA: Ross House Books, 2003), p. 201.

NOTES

NOTES

CHAPTER 8

DOMINION MANDATE

INTRODUCTION

In his book, *Magnalia Christi Americana*, Cotton Mather noted that three of the most significant events bearing on human affairs occurred less than one hundred years from one another: "the first was the resurrection of literature; the second was the opening of America; the third was the Reformation of Religion."[1] In 1450, the first Gutenberg printing press was created, the development of which eventually led to a revival of literacy, literature, and learning across Europe. Just forty-two years later in 1492, Columbus would sail to the New World, opening up new continents for eventual colonization. Twenty-five years after that, in 1517, Martin Luther would nail his Ninety-Five Theses to the chapel door at Wittenberg, and the Reformation would be under way. To those who lived at the time, each of these breakthroughs in all probability appeared as disconnected achievements by capable men who never knew each other. Yet for those like Mather who visualized the providential hand of God in history, these were the tools of dominion that Christ would use together to plant His own vineyard in the New World.

These elements did not immediately reach their full convergence. In 1517, it would have appeared unlikely that the New World would be dominated by the light of the Reformation. John Calvin, who is regarded by many as America's first founding father, was still a lad, just eight years of age. The three maritime powers were Spain, France, and England, each of which were Roman Catholic and loyal to the Pope. In 1494, the celebrated bull of Alexander VI had been issued "which divided the world in twain by a line drawn from pole to pole and bestowing on the Spanish sovereigns forever the dominion of the western hemisphere."[2] This papal bull "was interpreted in its fullest latitude. By virtue of its infallibility, the future kings of Spain claimed and maintained the right of jurisdiction in civil, political, and ecclesiastical affairs [in the New World]."[3] In 1519, a young Charles V would become the king of Spain and the beneficiary of this papal bequest. Charles was a devout Roman Catholic who would openly demonstrate his hostility to the Protestant Reformation during his confrontation of Luther at the Diet of Worms and by his urging of Pope Paul III to assemble the Council of Trent. By all indications, it would appear that the New World would be sealed off from the light of the Reformation.

Yet the fullness of time was soon realized, and pessimism would not prevail over God's work of providence. Throughout the remainder of the century, the walls would fall in around the Roman Pontiff. Rome with "its taxes and bureaucracy, property and prelates, its paralleling and sometimes dominating authority within the realm . . . was a constant irritant."[4] Consequently, Henry VIII, King of England, while not a supporter of the Protestant Reformation, declared the independence of the Church in England from Rome. In 1527, as devout as Emperor Charles V might have been, he too engaged in a reformation of sorts all of his own. It was in that year that the Duke of Bourbon, allied to the Charles V, would invade Rome and bring the Pope into captivity. As Otto Scott explains:

> In Madrid the Emperor publically denied his private pleasure by ordering prayers and processions for the pontiff's release: a release he could order at any time. His advisors talked about Spanish rule over Rome, and some thought 'that the Sacred Chair in Rome be . . . utterly and completely abolished.' Charles V withstood that temptation. To have his foot on the Pope now and in the future was sweet enough.[5]

The Roman monopoly had fallen; the seed of the Protestant Reformation had taken root in England—and the New World would reap the harvest. In 1559, the Protestant Elizabeth I ascended to the throne of England. During her reign, she relied greatly on Sir William Cecil who served as her chief advisor and Secretary of State. When in 1562 the topic of the New World was at issue, the Spanish ambassador reminded Cecil that the Papal Bull issued in 1494 granted the whole of the New World to Spain. Sir William Cecil responded that "the Pope had no right to partition the world and give and take kingdoms to whomever he pleased."[6]

Times had changed. Indeed, just forty-five years after Cecil made this statement, the first British Colony would be planted at Jamestown under the great seal of England.

One historian and adventurer, a contemporary of the Jamestown planting, said this of the English colonization of the New World, "That one main end of all these undertakings, was to plant the gospel in these dark regions of America."[7] This created a major distinction between the Spanish and the English models of colonization.[8] Spanish dominion was taken by crusade, as people, gold, and property were accumulated for the king by the force of arms. The English, by point of contrast, sought to colonize under the banner of gospel preaching, emphasizing liberty, industry, and private property. Consequently, the Spanish would send their soldiers to establish Spanish dominion in America, while the English would send strong families to plant Christ's dominion in America. The difference between the two was striking.

In this lecture, Doug Phillips will provide a historical overview of the Jamestown Colony. He will discuss the importance of the multigenerational vision and what it means to study the legacy that has been left to us by our forefathers. Mr. Phillips will also provide a number of character sketches of the faithful men and women who were used of God to overcome what seemed to be insurmountable odds. Finally, the history of Jamestown will come alive, as he discusses what the legacy of Jamestown means for us.

LECTURE OUTLINE: JAMESTOWN'S LEGACY OF LAW AND GOSPEL

I. **Introduction: Multigenerational Legacies**
   A. The heroic Frenchman Lafayette
   B. Israel Putnam
   C. John Adams and John Quincy Adams

II. **Ten Providences of God**
   A. The vision of Richard Hakluyt
   B. The displacement of the Spanish
   C. The establishment of the Reformation Christianity
   D. The preparation of John Smith
   E. The heart of Pocahontas
   F. The conversion and marriage of John Rolfe
   G. The coming of the *Deliverance*
   H. The establishment of the Christian Law
   I. The liberty of Edmund Sandys
   J. The courage of Nathaniel Bacon

III. **Jamestown: Land of Christian Firsts**
   A. First use of Christian common law
   B. First republican government
   C. First Christian church and thanksgiving
   D. First Christian conversions and baptisms
   E. First "interracial" marriage
   F. Firsts acts of lawful interposition against tyranny

IV. **Conclusions**
    A. The History of the Jamestown Celebrations (1807; 1857; 1907)
    B. John Quincy Adams's message on the 50th anniversary of Jamestown; the hand of Providence

QUESTIONS

1. Who was Israel Putnam?

2. What was the vision of Richard Hakluyt?

3. How was the life of John Smith prepared for the Jamestown Colony?

4. How was the marriage of John Rolfe with Pocahontas used by God?

5. What was the Bacon's Rebellion?

6. What was Bacon's fatal mistake?

7. What is it meant by Reformation Christianity?

8. What are some examples of the fact that Jamestown was a Christian establishment?

9. How did America change in the way it celebrates Jamestown's founding?

10. What is the heart of the message brought out in the quote by James Quincy Adams?

GROUP DISCUSSION/ASSIGNMENT

1. In William Bradford's *History of the Plymouth Settlement*, he speaks about a time when the settlement attempted to hold all land in common along with its produce. "The failure of this experiment on communal service," remarked Bradford, "proves the emptiness of the theory of Plato and of other ancients . . . that the taking away of private property, and the possession of it in community, by a common wealth, would make the state happy and flourishing; as if they were wiser than God. For in the instance community property so far as it went was found to breed much confusion and discontent, and retard much employment. . . . For the young men who were most able and fit for service objected to being forced to spend their time and strength working for other men's wives and children without any recompense."[9] Discuss this event in light of the modern welfare state.

2. Modern civilization is under the impression that trends in history move much more quickly in our modern times. They view change as taking place much more slowly than in past centuries. However, the settlers of Plymouth in 1620 (following Jamestown's establishment in 1607) came only ninety-nine years after Luther refused to recant his teachings at the Diet of Worms in 1521. Discuss the tremendous change that can take place in just under a century. Discuss the important role that Christians who have a multigenerational vision for

the future can play in the destiny of nations.

3. The Jamestown Colony created the Virginia House of Burgesses in 1619, establishing a republican form of government. In Plymouth, the colonists were particular to establish a representative form of government. However, in the Spanish colonies, the king of Spain mandated a strong centralized government in which virtually everything was managed from Madrid. Discuss the contract between these two governing styles and how they ended.

4. The seal of the Massachusetts Bay Colony had for its official seal an image of a North American Indian with the inscription, "Come Over and Help Us." This depicted the strong desire of the Puritans to evangelize the Indians. Their evangelistic efforts were largely successful through the work of Puritan missionaries such as John Eliot. Discuss this fact in light of many modern historians who prefer to paint the Puritans as hostile toward the Indians.

SCRIPTURE READINGS

Psalm 112

Matthew 28

FURTHER READING

The Mayflower Compact

In the name of God, Amen. We whose names are under-written, the loyal subjects of our dread sovereign Lord, King James, by the grace of God, of Great Britain, France, and Ireland King, Defender of the Faith, etc.

Having undertaken, for the glory of God, and advancement of the Christian faith, and honor of our King and Country, a voyage to plant the first colony in the northern parts of Virginia, do by these presents solemnly and mutually, in the presence of God, and one of another, covenant and combine our selves together into a civil body politic, for our better ordering and preservation and furtherance of the ends aforesaid; and by virtue hereof to enact, constitute, and frame such just and equal laws, ordinances, acts, constitutions and offices, from time to time, as shall be thought most meet and convenient for the general good of the Colony, unto which we promise all due submission and obedience. In witness whereof we have hereunder subscribed our names at Cape Cod, the eleventh of November [New Style, November 21], in the year of the reign of our sovereign lord, King James, of England, France, and Ireland, the eighteenth, and of Scotland the fifty-fourth. Anno Dom. 1620.

SCRIPTURE MEMORY

Isaiah 58:12, *"And they that shall be of thee shall build the old waste places: thou shalt raise up the foundations of many generations; and thou shalt be called, The repairer of the breach, The restorer of paths to dwell in."*

Jeremiah 29:5-6, *"Build ye houses, and dwell in them; and plant gardens, and eat the fruit of them; Take ye wives, and beget sons and daughters; and take wives for your sons, and give your daughters to husbands, that they may bear sons and daughters; that ye may be increased there, and not diminished."*

Nehemiah 4:14, *"And I looked, and rose up, and said unto the nobles, and to the rulers, and to the rest of the people, Be not ye afraid of them: remember the LORD, which is great and terrible, and fight for your brethren, your sons, and your daughters, your wives, and your houses."*

DEFINITIONS

Covenant: A compact or agreement between parties, the obligations of which are mutually binding.

Communion of Saints: All saints, that are united to Jesus Christ their Head, by His Spirit, and by faith, have fellowship with Him in His grace, sufferings, death, resurrection, and glory: and, being united to one another in love, they have communion in each other's gifts and graces, and are obliged to the performance of such duties, public and private, as do conduce to their mutual good, both in the inward and outward man. (Westminster Confession of Faith, Chapter 24)

Civil Magistrate: God, the supreme Lord and King of all the world, has ordained civil magistrates, to be, under Him, over the people, for His own glory, and the public good: and, to this end, has armed them with the power of the sword, for the defense and encouragement of them that are good, and for the punishment of evil doers. (Westminster Confession of Faith, Chapter 23)

SUMMARY

In Genesis 1:28, we learn that man was made in the image of God. Mankind is God's image bearer and is commanded to be fruitful and multiply and take dominion of the earth. The transplantation of godly men and women in the New World at Jamestown and Plymouth offers an incredible example for Christians today of the dominion mandate being rightly carried out. Moreover, the English model of dominion, which was centered around the family and liberty, provides a stark contrast to the Spanish model for dominion, which was centered around civil power and coercion.

The history of the colonization in the New World also provides a remedy to the faithless pessimism so prevalent in our modern Christian circles. That land, which explorers called the "New Jerusalem" and a "City on Hill", was settled in a time span less than a century after one of the darkest hours in world history.

Christians are commanded to be fruitful and multiply and take dominion of the earth in every age. The Christian must not only glean from the testimony of history as to this principle, but he must understand his place in history and embrace his responsibility to bear fruit for Christ's glory. A pessimistic view of history will cripple the observer not only from understanding the true testimony for history, but will also rob individuals of their true dominion purpose before the Lord.

BIBLIOGRAPHY

Of Plymouth Plantation, by William Bradford

Remarkable Providences Illustrative of the Earlier Days of American Colonization, by Increase Mather

Fearless Captain: Adventures of John Smith, by Aleck Loker

History of the Reformation, by J.H. Merle d'Aubigne

A Scottish Christian's Heritage, by Ian H Murray

The Reformation, by T.M. Lindsay

END NOTES

1. Cotton Mather, *Magnalia Christi Americana* (Carlisle, PA: Banner of Truth Trust, reprint 1979), p. 42.

2. Hubert H. Bancroft, *The Works of Hubert Howe Bancroft vol. xi* (San Francisco, CA: A.L. Bancroft & Co. Publishers, 1883), pp. 665-66.

3. *Ibid.*

4. Otto Scott, *The Great Christian Revolution* (Federal Way, WA: Uncommon Books, 1994), p. 20.

5. *Ibid.*, pp. 25-26.

6. Charles M. Andrews, *The Colonial Period of American History, Volume I* (New Haven, CT: Yale University Press, 1937), p. 20.

7. Mather, p. 45.

8. To learn more about these two distinctions, see: Dan Ford, *John Calvin and the Legacy of American Colonization* (St. Louis, MO: Lex Rex Publishing, 2009). Also see: Dan Ford "Competing Views of Dominion: Roman Catholic vs. Reformed", *Christianity & Western Civilization: Tracing 500 Years of the Influence of Christianity* (10 DVDs) (San Antonio, TX: Vision Forum, Inc., 2009).

9. William Bradford, *Of Plymouth Plantation* (San Antonio, TX: Vision Forum, Inc., reprint 2003), pp. 115-16.

NOTES

NOTES

CHAPTER 9

PROVIDENCE

INTRODUCTION

God governs every aspect of history in accordance with His eternal decrees issued before the foundation of the world. Though God transcends all time, space, and matter, He providentially directs the affairs of men to accomplish His divine goals. Nothing is beyond His purview or direction—from the smallest of creatures to the largest of empires. The study of history is thus the study of providence; it is the study of how God has orchestrated all of the facts of history for the good of those who are called according to His purpose (Rom. 8:28).

America, more than any other nation in our modern world, was established on the firm understanding that God was absolutely sovereign over the human affairs and that the providence of God could not be cut short or redirected by His creation. Christopher Columbus brought this view out with great clarity in his *Apologia*:

> *Our Lord wished to perform the clearest work of providence in this matter—the voyage to the Indies—to console me and others in this matter of the Holy Temple: I have spent seven years in the Royal Court arguing the case with many persons of such authority and learned in all the arts, and in the end they concluded that all was idle nonsense, and with this they gave up*

the enterprise; yet the outcome was to be the fulfillment of what our redeemer Jesus Christ
said beforehand through the mouth of the prophets.

Columbus believed that his discovery of the American continents was a work of divine providence. Though the most powerful and intellectual men who sat in the Spanish Royal Court at that time opposed the idea as idle nonsense, they could not divert God's providential purpose.

A solid understanding of the working of God's providence reverberates through the writing of America's Founders. John Adams wrote, "There is no such thing as human wisdom, all is the providence of God."[1] And later, "I always consider the settlement of America with reverence and wonder, as the opening of a grand scene and design in Providence for illumination of the ignorant, and the emancipation of the slavish part of mankind all over the earth."[2] During the debates for the adoption of the Federal Constitution, George Mason stated, "As nations cannot be rewarded or punished in the next world, they must be in this. By an inevitable chain of causes and effects, Providence punishes national sins, by national calamities."[3] George Washington, writing in 1788 about the ratification of the Constitution said, "No country upon earth ever had it more in its power to attain these blessings than United America. Wondrously strange, then, and much to be regretted indeed would it be, were we to neglect the means, and to depart from the road, which Providence has pointed out to us so plainly. I cannot believe it will ever come to pass. The great Governor of the universe has led us too long and too far on the road to happiness and glory, to forsake us in the midst of it."[4] The Founding Fathers of the American Republic interpreted history at large as well as their own place in history in light of God's sovereign work of providence.

Yet, for more than a century, the predominant leaders of Western culture have taken great pains to become religiously neutral in the public square and have rejected the idea of divine providence for a vain idea of self-providence. Modern evolution teaches that man lives in a world that is self-generated and self-sustaining. Therefore, for the evolutionist, he is utterly dependent on self-providence in a world that is driven by uncertainty. For most, even among those who profess Christianity, the idea of Divine Providence is considered a mere "personal belief", but no more. This has led to a wholesale abandonment of scriptural authority over civil government education, science, aesthetics, economics and all other fields dubbed as secular.

A similar rejection of Divine Providence is made when men declare neutrality over a particular area of life. To say that anything in the universe is neutral, or that God has left it to man's wisdom, is a rejection of God's sovereignty and work of Divine Providence in that area. However, "If God did indeed create heaven and earth and all things therein, then nothing can have meaning or interpretation apart from God. . . . The only true interpretation of any fact, including man, is in terms therefore of God the Creator and providential controller."[5] This means that neutrality does not and cannot exist. Education, science, aesthetics, economics, philosophy, psychology, and political science must all be seen as falling under God's total authority and care.

The Scriptures teach that all things are upheld by the power of God (Rom. 11:36; Col. 1:17; Heb. 1:3); that He works all things according to the counsel of His will (Dan. 4:34; Is. 46:9-11; Eph.1:11). Despite the boast of modern man of having evolved beyond God's governing hand, Israel's ancient King David declares otherwise in this remarkable description of the prideful scoffer, "For the Wicked boasteth of his heart's desire. . . . God is not in all his thoughts. . . . He hath said in his heart, God hath forgotten: he hideth his face; he will never see it." David's conclusion is definitive: "The LORD is King forever and ever: the heathen are perished out of his land" (Ps. 10:5-16).

In this lecture, Dr. Marshall Foster will discuss the inescapable importance of providence in history. He will show that the story of America's history is nothing shy of a miracle. He will also highlight statements made by leading founding fathers of our nation who saw the times they were living as being pregnant with purpose and who clearly trusted that the hand of providence would guide them. It is important, teaches Dr. Foster, that we look to the past to not only praise God for His miraculous work, but to understand that our time is likewise governed by His sovereign plan.

LECTURE OUTLINE: THE MIRACLE OF AMERICA

I.   **John Winthrop and America "City on a Hill"**

II. **God's Providence throughout History**
  A.   Definition of "Providence" from Noah Webster's 1828 Dictionary
  B.   God's protection from the French war ships in 1746
  C.   The common fasting and praying times during the colonial period
  D.   Technology used by God to accomplish His purpose
  E.   God's providence in the war against Hitler
  F.   Our Founding Fathers' view of Providence
  G.   The 1720 Depression
  H.   George Whitfield's sermons; the Great Awakening
  I.   The Defeat of the Spanish Armada
  J.   Patrick Henry's "Give me liberty or give me death" speech
  K.   God's protection from the Russians
  L.   God protects America from any attacks for 183 years
  M.   George Washington's view on providence
  N.   God's providence in the establishment of America

III. **The Gap between Generations**
  A.   Semantic infiltration
  B.   The pessimistic attitude
  C.   The wrong view of providence and miracles

IV. **Famous Quotes about God's Victory and Providence**
   A. John Owen
   B. John Calvin
   C. James Wendrook
   D. David Brainerd: Missionary to the American Indians
   E. Robert Moffat: Missionary to South Africa in 1816
   F. Charles Spurgeon: "The Prince of Preachers"
   G. Patrick Henry's words on his deathbed

V. **The Call for the Next Generation**

QUESTIONS

1. What is providence?

2. What was the state of the American colonies in 1720?

3. What man was used by God for the Great Awakening?

4. How were the French ships defeated?

5. What are some events through history that we see the clear hand of providence?

6. What was our Founding Fathers' view on providence?

7. What is semantic infiltration?

8. What does the pessimistic attitude say about our nation's present state?

9. What quote is Patrick Henry famous for?

10. What did all the quotes by famous Reformers have in common?

GROUP DISCUSSION/ASSIGNMENT

1. Many churchmen who ardently claim to believe in *Sola Scriptura* (Scripture Alone) prove to be ardent pragmatists when it comes to making everyday ethical decisions. One way this is manifested in our day is in how Christians approach voting decisions. While claiming to hold to a firm belief in the Scripture, when it comes to the practice of voting, they deny God's providence at the ballot box and instead attempt to assert their own work of providence by casting their votes for the so-called "lesser of two evils"—candidates who do not meet basic biblical qualifications for leadership. They seek to take the outcome of elections into their own hands, rather than obey God and leave the results to Him. Discuss how this approach is divergent from the Founders' views of providence and success.

2. The "God is dead" theology that was in vogue late in the last century did not teach that God is literally dead, but instead taught that He had become irrelevant and unnecessary in our every day decision-making. Even though most Christians would never openly assert such an absurdity,

many, in all practical terms, have fallen prey to this notion. Discuss how making decisions independent of the testimony of Scripture is tantamount to this heresy.

3. C.S. Lewis once observed that "the ancient man approached God (or even gods) as the accused person approaches his judge. For modern man, the roles are reversed. He is the judge: God is in the dock. . . . The trial may even end in God's acquittal. But the important thing is that man is on the bench and God is in the dock."[7] Discuss C. S. Lewis' comment in light of the testimony of America's Founders and the Reformers before them. Also discuss how this distinction plays a huge role in how we view the sovereignty of God.

4. In his well-known work, *Democracy in America*, Alexis de Tocqueville wrote, "The institutions of America which were a subject only of curiosity to monarchical France, ought to be the subject of study for republican France . . . whether it shall be . . . pacific or warlike, liberal or oppressive, a republic that menaces the sacred rights of property and family, or one that honors and protects them both. . . . Let us look to America." Ironically, while America was peaceful, France became warlike; while America was liberal, France was oppressive; and while America protected the rights to property and family, France sought to abolish them. One key difference was that America was founded on the principles of the Reformation, while France was founded on humanism. Discuss the fruits of America's reliance on the providence of God in contrast with the results of France's rejection of this doctrine.

SCRIPTURE READINGS

Job 38-40

Ephesians 1:1-14

FURTHER READING

The Westminster Confession of Faith on Providence

I. God the great Creator of all things does uphold, direct, dispose, and govern all creatures, actions, and things, from the greatest even to the least, by His most wise and holy providence, according to His infallible foreknowledge, and the free and immutable counsel of His own will, to the praise of the glory of His wisdom, power, justice, goodness, and mercy.

II. Although, in relation to the foreknowledge and decree of God, the first Cause, all things come to pass immutably, and infallibly; yet, by the same providence, He orders them to fall out, according to the nature of second causes, either necessarily, freely, or contingently.

III. God, in His ordinary providence, makes use of means, yet is free to work without, above, and against them, at His pleasure.

IV.   The almighty power, unsearchable wisdom, and infinite goodness of God so far manifest themselves in His providence, that it extends itself even to the first fall, and all other sins of angels and men; and that not by a bare permission, but such as has joined with it a most wise and powerful bounding, and otherwise ordering, and governing of them, in a manifold dispensation, to His own holy ends; yet so, as the sinfulness thereof proceeds only from the creature, and not from God, who, being most holy and righteous, neither is nor can be the author or approver of sin.

V.   The most wise, righteous, and gracious God does oftentimes leave, for a season, His own children to manifold temptations, and the corruption of their own hearts, to chastise them for their former sins, or to discover unto them the hidden strength of corruption and deceitfulness of their hearts, that they may be humbled; and, to raise them to a more close and constant dependence for their support upon Himself, and to make them more watchful against all future occasions of sin, and for sundry other just and holy ends.

VI.   As for those wicked and ungodly men whom God, as a righteous Judge, for former sins, does blind and harden, from them He not only withholds His grace whereby they might have been enlightened in their understandings, and wrought upon in their hearts; but sometimes also withdraws the gifts which they had, and exposes them to such objects as their corruption makes occasion of sin; and, withal, gives them over to their own lusts, the temptations of the world, and the power of Satan, whereby it comes to pass that they harden themselves, even under those means which God uses for the softening of others.

VII. As the providence of God does, in general, reach to all creatures; so, after a most special manner, it takes care of His Church, and disposes all things to the good thereof.

SCRIPTURE MEMORY

Daniel 2:20-21, "Daniel answered and said, Blessed be the name of God for ever and ever: for wisdom and might are his: And he changeth the times and the seasons: he removeth kings, and setteth up kings: he giveth wisdom unto the wise, and knowledge to them that know understanding."

Isaiah 55:8-11, "For my thoughts are not your thoughts, neither are your ways my ways, saith the LORD. For as the heavens are higher than the earth, so are my ways higher than your ways, and my thoughts than your thoughts. For as the rain cometh down, and the snow from heaven, and returneth not thither, but watereth the earth, and maketh it bring forth and bud, that it may give seed to the sower, and bread to the eater: So shall my word be that goeth forth out of my mouth: it shall not return unto me void, but it shall accomplish that which I please, and it shall prosper in the thing whereto I sent it."

Isaiah 14:24, 26-27, "The LORD of hosts hath sworn, saying, Surely as I have thought, so shall it come to pass; and as I have purposed, so shall it stand. . . . This is the purpose that is purposed upon the whole earth: and this is the hand that is stretched out upon all the nations. For the LORD of hosts hath purposed, and who shall disannul it? and his hand is stretched out, and who shall turn it back?"

Psalm 24:1-2, "The earth is the LORD's, and the fullness thereof; the world, and they that dwell therein. For he hath founded it upon the seas, and established it upon the floods."

Romans 8:28, "And we know that all things work together for good to them that love God, to them who are the called according to his purpose."

DEFINITIONS

The Myth of Neutrality: The myth that there are spheres over which God has no control or prescribes no ethical rule of conduct.

Spheres of Sovereignty: All authority is derivative and has its origin in God alone. God has delegated authority to four institutions which are separate spheres of jurisdiction: the family, the civil government, the church, and the individual.

Providence: The care and superintendence that God exercises over His creatures.

> *God the great Creator of all things does uphold, direct, dispose, and govern all creatures, actions, and things, from the greatest even to the least, by His most wise and holy providence, according to His infallible foreknowledge, and the free and immutable counsel of His own will, to the praise of the glory of His wisdom, power, justice, goodness, and mercy. (Westminster Confession of Faith, Ch. V:1)*

SUMMARY

One of the major problems with culture today is that Christians do not truly believe in Providence. This has led to pragmatism and compromise—to our salt losing its savor. This error is common among historians who prefer to use the terms "chance" or "luck" rather than give glory to God for His works of providence.

The Christian historian must look at history in terms of how God has providentially worked out the details of history in accordance with His good pleasure. All human action must be interpreted with reference to the will of God alone, and not that of the creature. It is hypocritical to confess with our lips that God upholds the universe according to His will, but then act as if some things are upheld by the power of man's will and ability.

BIBLIOGRAPHY

Liberty Order, and Justice, by James McClellan

The Reformation of Rights, by John Witte, Jr.

The Genevan Reformation and the American Founding, by David W. Hall

From Terror to Triumph, by Dr. Marshall Foster

Christianity and the American Commonwealth, by Charles Galloway

For You They Signed, by Marilyn Boyer

END NOTES

1. John Adams and Charles Francis Adams, *The Works of John Adams, Vol. III* (Boston, MA: Little, Brown, and Company, 1865), p. 191.

2. *Ibid.*, p. 452.

3. James Madison, *Debates on the Adoption of the Federal Constitution* (Washington, D.C.: Congress, 1845), p. 558.

4. Jared Sparks, *The Writings of George Washington, Vol. IX* (Boston, MA: Russell, Odiorne, & Metcafe, 1835), pp. 391-92.

5. R.J. Rushdoony, *By What Standard* (Vallecito, CA: Ross House Books, 1995), p. 9.

6. Psalm 10:5-11,16

7. C.S. Lewis, "God on the Dock", in Walter Hooper, ed., *God on the Dock: Essays on Theology and Ethics* (Grand Rapids, MI: Eerdmans, 1970), p. 244.

NOTES

CHAPTER 10

THE FAMILY

INTRODUCTION

The family is the only human institution that God established in the perfection of Eden. The family survived mankind's expulsion from the Garden, and it has been at the center of every Divine Covenant that God has made with man ever since. The Edenic and Noahic Covenants, along with their dominion mandates, were made with the heads of families with the command to be fruitful and multiply and replenish the earth. The Abrahamic, Mosaic, and Land Covenants not only were made effectual through families, but laid the covenantal basis for all education and law. The Davidic Covenant established the royal family of David on the throne of Israel, through which Christ was heir. The New Covenant was established by God the Father through the atoning sacrifice of His Son Jesus Christ, and it is offered to all those who receive the adoption of sons.

The family is also the cornerstone of all other legitimate human institutions. Dr. B.M. Palmer stated:

> *By the co-existence of many households society at large may be constituted. The family*
> *may be viewed . . . as the original society from which the states emerge and the church, and*
> *every other association known among men. . . . Neither State nor Church could exist, but*
> *of the material which the Family affords.*[1]

Cotton Mather also drew this connection, writing, "It is evident that families are the nurseries of all societies. . . . Well ordered families, naturally produce a good order in other societies." With regard to the church, Mather agreed with another author who wrote, "If parents did their duties as they ought, the Word publicly preached would not be the ordinary means of regeneration in the church, also outside the church, among the infidels."[2] When it comes to the good ordering of society, the institution of the family comes first.

Throughout world history, the greatest works of providence have been accompanied with a revival of the biblical family. In fact, Scripture clearly declares that such a revival of the biblical family took place just prior to the coming of Christ. "Behold, I will send you Elijah the prophet before the coming of the great and dreadful day of the LORD," declared the Prophet Micah, "And he shall turn the heart of the fathers to the children, and the heart of the children to their fathers, lest I come and smite the earth with a curse." (Malachi 4:5-6) Where ever the biblical family is strong, the providential blessings of liberty, prosperity, and felicity will follow.

In contrast to this truth, evolutionary sociology maintains that the family and marriage is an antiquated convention formed by primitive societies in order to care for children. Modern socialism in these United States and abroad has thereby devalued the family and sought to utterly destroy it. For the socialist, children belong to the State, which, in their view, provides a better means of caring for children. The family is therefore no longer needed. Socialist H.G. Wells admits, "Socialism repudiates the private ownership of the head of the family as completely as it repudiates any other sort of ownership. . . . [I]t intervenes between the children and the parents, claiming to support them, protect them, and educate them for its own ampler purposes. Socialism, in fact, is the State family. The old family of the private individual must vanish away."[3]

In recent times, the biblical family has in large part been abandoned by Western culture, even among those who profess Christianity. Modern man has sought to replace the biblical family established in Eden with a weak form of cohabitation. Compulsory education, no-fault divorce, symbolic speech, feminism, abortion, homosexuality, and the property and estate tax are all modern trends that have been advanced to deteriorate the biblical family. The secular humanist social engineers of the twentieth century understood that the Christian family is the seed of Christian culture; that to destroy the Christian family is to destroy Christian culture.

The family is the cornerstone to every other human institution. The home is the primary place of worship, the primary institution for education, and the primary hall of liberty and justice. If the family is destroyed, then life, liberty, and property are generally destroyed along with it. The fight for the family is thus the fight for civilization.

The family has been a key instrument used by God to accomplish His purpose throughout history, and if Christians are serious about changing culture today, they must reject the modern humanist model for the family and embrace the biblical model of the family instead.

In this lecture, Dr. Marshall Foster will discuss the import role that the family has played throughout history. He will explain that there is no authority outside from God; all authority is derivative, finding its origin in God. Dr. Foster will demonstrate that strong civilizations and strong churches follow a strong family. He will conclude by calling all Christians to begin turning their hearts to their families.

LECTURE OUTLINE: HOW FAMILIES CHANGED THE WORLD

I. **The Battle of the Dynasties: 1603 Dynasty of the Devil Met the Dynasty of God**
   A. Dynasty of the Devil
      1. James VI of Scotland becomes James I of England
      2. Persecutes Christians
      3. Bankrupts his country
      4. Poisoned by his own family
   B. Dynasty of God
      1. Christians, covenant families
      2. Sent to Holland
      3. Mayflower departure (1620)
      4. Plymouth Colony

II. **The Impact of Christian Families Faithfulness**

III. **The Unstoppable Strategy of God**
   A. The Individual Redeemed (Matt. 28:20)
   B. The Family Dynasty (Deut. 7:9)
   C. The Local Church (Matt. 16:18)
   D. Limited Civil Government (Rom. 13)

IV. **The Dominion Mandate**
   A. The dominion commission given to Adam and Eve (Gen. 1:26-30)
   B. The meaning of the "Dominion Mandate" (Francis Nigel Lee)

V. **Family Dynasties**
   A. The judgment of illegitimate dynasties
   B. The blessings for godly dynasties
   C. The way to discern illegitimate dynasties
   D. Types of unfaithful dynasties

VI. **The Family Dynasty Basic Plan (the "Shema")-Deuteronomy 6:4-10**
   A. Know who God is
   B. Love God
   C. Teach God's truth to your children
   D. Obey God's law

E. Expect great blessings to you and your children to one thousand generations

VII. God-Directed Spheres of Authority

A. Family (Gen. 1:26-28; Prov. 22:6)

1. Procreation
2. Economics (Business)
3. Education
4. Social Welfare
5. Tithing
6. Hospitality
7. Model of Union with Christ

B. Church (Gen. 12:3; Eph. 4)

1. Training of the Saints
2. Reflecting God's unity
3. Corporate worship
4. Disciple
5. Caring for widows and orphans
6. Preparing the body for warfare

C. State (Gen. 9:6; Rom. 13)

1. Punishing the law breakers
2. Protecting the righteous, freeing them for good works

VIII. Conclusions

A. Church in the Roman Empire was built from the beginning on families
B. Men need to be willing to sacrifice for their families
C. Family dynasties built Western Civilization
D. Theologians, scholars, and missionaries transformed cultures

QUESTIONS

1. What dynasties were used by God to create a great nation?

2. What is it meant by "Dominion Mandate"?

3. How do we discern illegitimate dynasties?

4. Name some illegitimate dynasties and their affect on history.

5. What is the Family Dynasty basic plan?

6. What are God-directed spheres of authority?

7. What are some of the duties of the family?

8. What are some of the duties of the church?

9. What are some of the duties of the state?

10. How did the transformation in good cultures take place?

GROUP DISCUSSION/ASSIGNMENT

1. In his book, *The Little Boy Down the Road*, Doug Phillips wrote this about the modern war on fathers, "Patricide is the act of killing fathers. Revisionist history is a form of patricide, when historians attack the spiritual forefather of a nation, or when they pervert the legacies of the past, they engage in a form of cultural patricide."[4] Discuss the importance of history in light of the legacy of fathers. Discuss why any study of history is a study of multigenerational faithfulness.

2. The family has been called the first school, the first communion of worship, the first body politic. Discuss how the family is central to every human institution.

3. Deuteronomy 6 not only makes it clear that parents are responsible for the education of children, but it also makes clear the religious nature that education must assume. Discuss why it is important for parents to obey the Scriptures and take the responsibility of education their own children.

4. The biblical model for the family goes back to the creation itself. A husband is clearly to take the leadership role in the family. In Genesis 3:16, God tells Eve, "Thy desire shall be to thy husband, and he shall rule over thee." Later, when explaining why women should not teach or have authority over a man, Paul states, "For Adam was first formed, then Eve." Feminism, however, has done much to disrupt this order of creation and has sought to remove any trace that a wife should be under the authority of her husband. Discuss why it is important for the Christian to reject the lies of feminism in order to reclaim the biblical family.

SCRIPTURE READINGS

Ephesians 6

1 Corinthians 11

Colossians 3

FURTHER READING

John Bunyan: Duties of the Master of Families

First, As touching the spiritual state of his family; he ought to be very diligent and circumspect, doing his utmost endeavour both to increase faith where it is begun, and to begin it where it is not.

Wherefore, to this end, he ought diligently and frequently to lay before his household such things of God, out of his word, as are suitable for each particular. And let no man question his rule in the word of God for such a practice; for if the thing itself were but of good report, and a thing tending to civil honesty, it is within the compass and bounds even of nature itself, and ought to be done; much more things of a higher nature; besides, the apostle exhorts us to 'Whatsoever things are honest, whatsoever things are just, pure, lovely, and of good report, to think of them,' that is, to be mindful to do them (Phil 4:8). But to be conversant in this godly exercise in our family, is very worthy of praise, and doth much become all Christians. This is one of the things for which God so highly commended his servant Abraham, and that with which his heart was so much affected. I know Abraham, saith God, 'I know him' to be a good man in very deed, for 'he will command his children, and his household after him, and they shall keep the way of the Lord' (Gen 18:19). This was a thing also which good Joshua designed should be his practice as long as he had a breathing time in this world. 'As for me,' saith he, I 'and my household, we will serve the Lord' (Josh 24:15).

Further, we find also in the New Testament, that they are looked upon as Christians of an inferior rank that have not a due regard to this duty; yea, so inferior as not fit to be chosen to any office in the church of God. A [bishop or] pastor must be one that ruleth well his own house, having his children in subjection with all gravity; For if a man know not how to rule his own house, how shall he take care of the church of God? 'The deacon' also, saith he, must 'be the husband of one wife, ruling their children, and their own house well' (1 Tim 3). Mark a little, the apostle seems to lay down thus much, that a man that governs his family well, hath one qualification belonging to a pastor or deacon in the house of God, for he that knoweth not how to rule his own house, how shall he take care of the church of God? which thing considered, it giveth us light into the work of the master of a family, touching the governing of his house.

1. A pastor must be sound and incorrupt in his doctrine; and indeed so must the master of a family (Titus 1:9; Eph. 6:4).

2. A pastor should be apt to teach, to reprove, and to exhort; and so should the master of a family (1 Tim 3:2; Deut. 6:7).

3. A pastor must himself be exemplary in faith and holiness; and so also should the master of a family (1 Tim 3:2-4; 4:12). 'I,' saith David, 'will behave myself in a perfect way; I will walk in,' or before, 'my house with a perfect heart' (Psalm 101:2).

4. The pastor is for getting the church together; and when they are so come together, then to pray among them, and to preach unto them. This is also commendable in Christian masters of families.

SCRIPTURE MEMORY

Malachi 2:14-15, "Yet ye say, Wherefore? Because the LORD hath been witness between thee and the wife of thy youth, against whom thou hast dealt treacherously: yet is she thy companion, and the wife of thy covenant. And did not he make one? Yet had he the residue of the spirit. And wherefore one? That he might seek a godly seed. Therefore take heed to your spirit, and let none deal treacherously against the wife of his youth."

Exodus 20:12, "Honour thy father and thy mother: that thy days may be long upon the land which the LORD thy God giveth thee."

Genesis 2:22-24, "And the rib, which the LORD God had taken from man, made he a woman, and brought her unto the man. And Adam said, This is now bone of my bones, and flesh of my flesh: she shall be called Woman, because she was taken out of Man. Therefore shall a man leave his father and his mother, and shall cleave unto his wife: and they shall be one flesh."

DEFINITIONS

Multigenerational: The idea that vision is to be passed from one generation to the next.

Family Worship: The act of worshiping God in the home among the members of the family.

Patriarchy: The biblical view of the family in which Christ is the head of the home; the husband has authority over his wife, and the children are in subjection to their parents.

SUMMARY

The family has historically been the cradle of all human institutions. It is the bedrock of civilization, the green house of culture, the undergirding strength of industry, the torch of learning, and the nerve center of all human progress. The family is also the chief catalyst for discipleship, the daily propagator of orthodoxy, an abundant spring of philanthropy, the primary seat of worship, and an effectual incubator of orthopraxy.

For the historian, the family is of utmost importance. Not only do the greatest movements of God follow a revival of the family, but without the family there would be very little to draw history together. History is carried on the wings of strong families. Those who fail to look to their forefathers who have run the good race before them are ignorant of the ancient landmarks and become uprooted from the past. Moreover, fathers who fail to pass on a faithful legacy to their children through diligent discipleship have no hope for the future.

BIBLIOGRAPHY

The Family, by B.M. Palmer and J.W. Alexander

Family Reformation, by Scott T. Brown

The 200-Year Plan: A Practicum on Multigenerational Faithfulness (12 CDs), by Doug Phillips and Geoffrey Botkin

A Family Well Ordered, by Cotton Mather

The Mathers, by Robert Middlekauff

Courtship, Engagement and Marriage, by John Witte Jr. and Robert M. Kingdon

The Family, by J.R. Miller

END NOTES

1. B.M. Palmer, *The Family* (Harrisonburg, VA: Sprinkle Publication, reprint 1991), p. 9.

2. Cotton Mather, *A Family Well-Ordered* (Morgan, PA: Soli Deo Gloria Publications, reprint 2001), pp. 1-2.

3. H.G. Wells, *Socialism and the Family* (London: A.C. Fifield Publisher, 1906), pp. 29-30.

4. Doug Phillips, *The Little Boy Down the Road* (San Antonio, TX: Vision Forum, Inc., 2008), p. 139.

NOTES

ABOUT THE AUTHOR

Elijah Brown resides in Virginia with his wife, Camellia Oana Brown, and is the father of four children. He earned his Juris Doctor degree in 2009 from Oak Brook College of Law and Public Policy and works full time in the area of family advocacy.